THE BLACK EXPERIENCE
IN THE CIVIL WAR SOUTH

THE BLACK EXPERIENCE
IN THE CIVIL WAR SOUTH

STEPHEN V. ASH

Reflections on the Civil War Era
John David Smith, Series Editor

 PRAEGER

AN IMPRINT OF ABC-CLIO, LLC
Santa Barbara, California • Denver, Colorado • Oxford, England

Library of Congress Cataloging-in-Publication Data

Ash, Stephen V.
   The Black experience in the Civil War South / Stephen V. Ash.
      p. cm. — (Reflections on the Civil War era)
   Includes bibliographical references and index.
   ISBN 978-0-275-98524-0 (alk. paper) — ISBN 978-0-313-04204-1 (ebook)
1. African Americans—Southern States—History—19th century.   2. Slaves—
Southern States—History—19th century.   3. Slavery—Southern States—
History—19th century.   4. Slaves—Emancipation—Southern States.
5. Plantation life—Southern States—History—19th century.   6. Southern
States—Social conditions—19th century.   I. Title.
   E185.18.A84   2010
   973.70896—dc22   2009051217

ISBN: 978-0-275-98524-0
EISBN: 978-0-313-04204-1

14   13   12   11   10   1   2   3   4   5

This book is also available on the World Wide Web as an eBook.
Visit www.abc-clio.com for details.

Praeger
An Imprint of ABC-CLIO, LLC

ABC-CLIO, LLC
130 Cremona Drive, P.O. Box 1911
Santa Barbara, California 93116-1911

This book is printed on acid-free paper ∞

Manufactured in the United States of America

To
Michael L. "Mike" Miles, 1952–2009
Beloved kinsman and friend

CONTENTS

SERIES FOREWORD

"Like Ol' Man River," the distinguished Civil War historian Peter J. Parish wrote in 1998, "Civil War historiography just keeps rolling along. It changes course occasionally, leaving behind bayous of stagnant argument, while it carves out new lines of inquiry and debate."

Since Confederate General Robert E. Lee's men stacked their guns at Appomattox Court House in April 1865, historians and partisans have been fighting a war of words over the causes, battles, results, and broad meaning of the internecine conflict that cost more than 620,000 American lives. Writers have contributed between 50,000 and 60,000 books and pamphlets on the topic. Viewed in terms of defining American freedom and nationalism, western expansion and economic development, the Civil War quite literally launched modern America. "The Civil War," Kentucky poet, novelist, and literary critic Robert Penn Warren explained, "is for the American imagination, the great single event of our history. Without too much wrenching, it may, in fact, be said to *be* American history."

The books in Praeger's *Reflections on the Civil War Era* series examine pivotal aspects of the American Civil War. Topics range from examinations of military campaigns and local conditions, to analyses of institutional, intellectual, and social history. Questions of class, gender, and race run through each volume in the series. Authors, veteran experts in their respective fields, provide concise, informed, readable syntheses—fresh looks at familiar topics with new source material and original arguments.

"Like all great conflicts," Parish noted in 1999, "the American Civil War reflected the society and the age in which it was fought." Books in *Reflections on the Civil War Era* interpret the war as a salient event in the hammering out and understanding of American identity before, during, and after the secession crisis of 1860–1861. Readers will find the volumes valuable guides as they chart the troubled waters of mid-nineteenth-century American life.

John David Smith
Charles H. Stone Distinguished Professor of American History
The University of North Carolina at Charlotte

PREFACE AND ACKNOWLEDGMENTS

In the 1860s a great war was fought in America and slavery was abolished. Nearly every American today knows something of these momentous events, for the Civil War is very much a part of our national consciousness. But the public understanding of what the nation experienced between 1861 and 1865 is monopolized by bloody battles and exalted leaders: Shiloh and Gettysburg, Lincoln and Lee, and the rest. These famous events and celebrated people were enormously important, to be sure, but they are not the whole story of the Civil War.

This book deals with other events and other people, of enormous importance collectively but individually obscure and anonymous. It is about the black people who lived in the Southern states during the war, about what they did, what was done to them, and what they thought about their experience.

While the general public is unfamiliar with this subject, professional historians are not. Many books have been written about it, especially in the last four decades. But almost all of these focus on a particular state or region or community, or a particular segment of the black population, or a particular aspect of the black experience. This book is intended to be comprehensive. It tells not only of blacks in the Confederate states but also of those in the Southern states that remained in the Union, not only of those on farms and plantations but also of those in towns and cities, not only of those who were slaves when the war began but also of those who were free, and not only of black men but also of black women and children.

Most significantly, this book tells not only of those who gained freedom during the war but also of those who did not. In this it stands apart from other works on the wartime black experience published in recent decades, most of which portray the war years primarily as a time of liberation, or at least as a time of loosening of the bonds of slavery. This emphasis, while fairly depicting the experience of many blacks, obscures the experience of many more.

When the Confederate armies surrendered in the spring of 1865 most Southern blacks were in the same position they had been in four years earlier: they were enslaved—held as property and thoroughly subject to their master's will. This was so, as the first chapter of this book explains, mainly because Southern whites were determined to keep blacks in bondage, and in most parts of the South they maintained the power to do so until the Confederate government and armies were wholly extinguished and Union authority prevailed throughout the Southern states, a gradual process that extended well into the summer of 1865. An aged former slave in Texas, interviewed in the 1930s, made this point succinctly. "It's a funny thing how folks always want to know about the War," said Felix Haywood. "The war weren't so great as folks suppose. Sometimes you didn't knowed it was goin' on. It was the endin' of it that made the difference."[1]

That most Southern blacks began and ended the war as slaves does not mean they were untouched by the great events of 1861 to 1865. As the second and third chapters of this book show, they experienced many changes in their lives. But only a minority of Southern blacks, those discussed in chapters 4 and 5, broke free of the bonds of slavery in any meaningful way before the war's end.

This book focuses on what the black people in the Civil War South experienced personally, that is, how their lives were touched by wartime events. Two related matters that have interested historians receive little or no attention here, and readers should look elsewhere to learn about them. The movement within the Confederacy to reform the institution of slavery generated considerable discussion among whites and revealed much about white beliefs regarding slavery and the meaning of the war, but it resulted in no concrete reforms and had virtually no impact on the slaves themselves. Likewise, the late-war movement to recruit slaves as Confederate soldiers, while richly revelatory about white racial and nationalistic ideology, was manifested primarily in debate among whites and directly affected no more than a handful of blacks. White attitudes toward blacks are by no means ignored in this book, however. Where such attitudes had real consequences in blacks' lives—for example, the white fear of slave rebellion, which led to the tightening of racial controls and redoubled violence against blacks—they are duly discussed in these pages.

It is a pleasure to acknowledge here the assistance of those who helped bring this book to fruition. John David Smith, the series editor, is the very model of what such an editor should be: encouraging, insightful, and helpful. Several of my friends in the History profession provided valuable sources or information; Dean Thomas and John Stealey deserve special mention. The University of Tennessee made available research time and library resources without which I could not have completed the project, while my colleagues in the History Department offered congenial company and astute commentary. My greatest debt is to my family, who provided the essential things.

INTRODUCTION

The muscle and sweat and skills of black people of African descent helped build the Old South, but they reaped few rewards from their labor. By 1860 they numbered 4,200,000, spread unevenly across the South (the 15 U.S. states where slavery was legal) but comprising, over all, one-third of the region's population. Some were artisans such as carpenters or blacksmiths, some were maids or butlers or cooks or carriage drivers, but most were field hands whose labor produced the bulk of the South's great cash crops of cotton, rice, sugar, and tobacco. Some lived in towns or cities, some on small farms, but most lived on large plantations among 20 or 50 or even 100 or more other black men, women, and children. A small proportion, 6 of every 100, were free, but all the rest were slaves who could be, and frequently were, bought and sold just like cotton or cattle.[1]

Southern slavery was a harsh system—cruel is a better word—that was now and then tempered by acts of kindness on the part of paternalistic whites. As far as most slaveowners were concerned, slaves existed solely to make a profit for them and to ease the burden of housework and other chores. Slaves were expected to obey their masters without question, and few masters hesitated to punish misbehavior. Such punishment was usually corporal: the sound of a whip lacerating a black back was common in the Old South. The more serious forms of slave resistance were answered not only with the whip but sometimes with the gallows.

The vast majority of enslaved people hated slavery and longed to be free. But faced with whites' determination to subjugate them and with the array of laws, institutions, and sheer physical force that gave whites the power to do so, slaves rarely dared to challenge the system. Outright rebellions were very few and never successful. Some slaves ran away from their masters, but almost all were soon recaptured. The only sort of resistance that most slaves could get away with was the quiet sort: feigning sickness or stupidity, "accidentally" breaking tools or dishes, and laughing at their masters' foibles behind their backs.

Most slaves just resigned themselves, reluctantly, to getting along in the cruel and unjust system that held them captive. They did what their masters told them to do and accepted whatever kindness was extended to them, but without the cheerful willingness and gratitude that their masters expected. Moreover, they softened the rigors of bondage and made their servitude endurable by embracing and nurturing family life, community life, and spiritual life. In the slave quarters of the plantations, and elsewhere throughout the rural and urban South, enslaved men and women fell in love, married, had children, and gathered with others whenever they could to gossip, sing, celebrate, and worship. Often joining in this fellowship were free blacks, who, although they answered to no master and could not be bought or sold, were so hemmed in by racially restrictive laws and customs that they enjoyed only a quasi-freedom.

Few white Southerners in 1860 had any qualms about slavery, and most gave little thought to how the slaves felt about it. But by that time many Americans outside the South had turned against the institution. Some, stirred by sympathy for the slave and hatred of the "sin" of slaveholding, were outright abolitionists, demanding that the South do away with its "peculiar institution." Many more were free-soilers, content to let slavery continue in the South but determined that it not spread into the developing western frontier. In the four decades prior to 1860, American politics was repeatedly shaken by clashes between antislavery Northerners and proslavery Southerners. Compromises smoothed things over time and again, but in 1860 further compromise became impossible.

In November of that year, Abraham Lincoln, a Northerner who stood immovably on the free-soil platform of the Republican party, won the presidential election. Facing the prospect of an administration hostile to slavery, most whites in the seven Deep South states concluded that leaving the Union was the only way to ensure slavery's survival. By February 1861 those states had seceded and formed the Confederate States of America. In April, following President Lincoln's refusal to give up the U.S. Army's Fort Sumter in the harbor of Charleston, South Carolina, Confederate military forces bombarded the fort. Lincoln immediately declared his intention to put down the Southern "rebellion" and called on the loyal states for troops. Four Upper South states subsequently seceded and joined the Confederacy. On both sides, men volunteered for military service by the tens of thousands and began massing into great armies. And so the war came.

Most blacks, even in the remotest parts of the South, on the most isolated farms and plantations, were aware of these momentous developments and followed them intently. Much of what they learned, however, was filtered through the perceptions of whites. John Majors, a slave in northern Mississippi, listened during the secession crisis whenever his master chatted with friends in the marketplace or outside the courthouse in Oxford. Often the talk was about the possibility of war; as Majors recalled, the consensus was that "hit wont be much of a war if dey has any at all, jes take two or three months to whip de damn Yankees an' teach dem to tend to dey own business an' let de folks down South alone."[2] Once the war was under way, many slaves went with their masters to watch the volunteers muster and drill and to hear the patriotic speeches at flag-presentation ceremonies. Some masters simply told their slaves what they thought they ought to know. Late in 1861, for instance, all 350 slaves on one of the huge estates in the South Carolina lowcountry assembled in the plantation church at their master's beckoning and listened as he warned them that the evil Yankees were invading the South bent on mayhem.[3]

There were many things going on that masters did not want their slaves to know, and they did their best to suppress or censor or distort such dangerous news. It helped that almost all slaves were illiterate. But slaves had always had ways of gaining forbidden knowledge and communicating it among themselves, and in the tumultuous months of secession and war this "grapevine telegraph," as they called it, was humming.[4] One evening in April 1861, 13-year-old William Robinson of North Carolina, a house boy, served whiskey to his master and a half dozen other men who had gathered in his home; later, disobeying an order to go to bed, Robinson tip-toed down from his upstairs room and listened through the keyhole of a closed door as the men discussed the firing on Fort Sumter and the war that was now sure to follow. Slaves on the Bouldin plantation in Washington County, Texas, slipped away from their quarters many a night and took position beneath an open window of the Big House, where they could overhear the white family discussing the war's progress.[5] The few slaves who could read sometimes perused newspapers surreptitiously or peeked at their master's personal correspondence and thereby gained illicit knowledge. However they acquired the news, slaves spread it rapidly among themselves. "Whenever we met," recalled Thomas Johnson of Richmond, "all our talk would be about what we had heard."[6] Henry Clay Bruce of Missouri described how "from mouth to ear the news was carried from farm to farm, without the knowledge of masters."[7]

As they eagerly but quietly gathered news about secession and war and talked it over among themselves, most slaves developed the very convictions and aspirations that their masters feared most. They quickly came to believe that Northerners were their friends and allies, that the North was fighting to free the slaves, and that a Northern victory would shatter the chains that bound them. Ironically, they got these impressions not from the words or actions of President Lincoln or other U.S. officials (who in the early part of the war made it clear that they intended only to restore the Union and had no intention of meddling with slavery) but from their own masters and other Southern whites, who scoffed at Lincoln's public denials and insisted that his armies were advancing southward to make war on slavery.[8] Young William Robinson, listening at the keyhole that night in April 1861, distinctly heard one of his master's friends say that "if the Yankees whipped [us], every negro would be free."[9] The 350 South Carolina slaves who gathered in their plantation church later that year were told by their master that the Northern invaders "would try and induce them to desert."[10]

These early rumors that the Yankee invaders were brandishing the banner of emancipation struck a special chord in the hearts of many slaves. Millennial expectations, encouraged especially by their understanding of the Old Testament, had long buoyed the spirits of the black men and women of the South. Freedom would come one day, many devoutly believed—if not for this generation then perhaps the next.[11] Jacob Stroyer of South Carolina remembered hearing, as a little boy during "the dark days of slavery" in the 1850s, his father comforting his mother with the words, "the time will come when this boy and the rest of the children will be their own masters and mistresses."[12] The Civil War seemed to many to herald that long-awaited Year of Jubilee. In wartime Richmond, Thomas Johnson, one of the rare slaves who could read, met secretly with other slaves and read to them from the Bible to try to make sense of the uncertain times. They were struck especially by Daniel 11:15: "So the king of the north shall come . . . and the arms of the south shall not withstand."[13]

Quietly slaves prayed for Northern victory. Their prayers grew more fervent as the war went on and Union policy evolved to embrace emancipation. By 1863 it was certain that a Yankee triumph would usher in the Year of Jubilee; it went without saying, of course, that a Rebel triumph would postpone it.[14] In Athens, Georgia, a woman sat, Sunday after Sunday, with her fellow slaves in the gallery of the First Presbyterian Church. As the white minister prayed aloud "that the Lord would drive the Yankees back," she prayed silently, "Oh, Lord, please send the Yankees on and let them set us free."[15]

As the war news turned grim for the Confederacy and Union victory became more likely, many slaves grew jubilant. On Jacob Stroyer's plantation, Christmas of 1864 "was the greatest which had ever been to the slaves," for even though they were still unfree "we felt that the chains which had bound us so long were well nigh broken."[16] Slaves tried to conceal their excitement, of course, but some of the more perceptive whites were undeceived. "I believe the darkies all think this is a crisis in their lives that must be taken advantage of," wrote a South Carolina plantation lady. "Times and slaves have changed since the [beginning of this] revolution."[17]

The prayers of slaves and the prophecies of the Old Testament might ensure Union victory, but no one could be certain of that. After all, Southern whites were praying just as hard that God would smite the Yankee hosts, and they could point to comforting Bible passages of their own. And as long as Confederate armies survived to contest the enemy's advance, whites were determined to preserve slavery. When the war brought new challenges to the institution, whites rose to meet them.

ONE

FREEDOM DELAYED

Whatever the dreams and expectations of Southern blacks in the tumultuous time of secession and war, their actual experience was shaped to a considerable extent by those who held power over them. These included not just the slaveowners (a minority of the white population) but also the white community as a whole, along with institutions of government and law.

Southern whites may not have agreed on much else, but they were virtually unanimous in their belief that enslaving blacks was necessary and proper. They found justification in their reading of history and the Bible and in their day-to-day interactions with blacks. It seemed obvious to them that blacks were a feckless, ignorant, inferior race, unable to control or support themselves and thus in need of governance and nurturance by the superior white race. "Experience proves that they require the aid of the white man to work out their civilization," wrote a South Carolinian in the spring of 1861, "& that even when this is in a measure, attained, they relapse again into barbarism as soon as that aid is withdrawn. It is only whilst under the guidance of the white man, & in his service that they have ever made any progress."[1] As this quotation suggests, whites envisaged slavery as a boon to the slave as well as the master. A white Texan explained that "His [the Negro's] happiest position is *Chattel Slavery*, where he is directed and compelled to labor in health, [and] cared for in sickness and decrepitude."[2] Most slaveowners, although certainly not all, took seriously the responsibility of caring for their bondsmen, but they expected them to labor faithfully in return. As they frequently reminded them, the Bible itself enjoined such fidelity. Among many such verses that masters cited was Colossians 3:22: "Servants, obey in all things your masters . . . ; not with eyeservice, as menpleasers; but in singleness of heart, fearing God."[3]

As whites proclaimed the righteousness of slavery, they also proclaimed their determination to defend the institution from the wicked designs of fanatical Northerners. In December 1860, a few weeks after Lincoln's election, citizens of Cooke County, Texas, assembled to discuss the crisis. The now-dominant Republican party, they declared, was clearly bent on "extinguishing negro slavery in the Southern States at all hazards, however unscrupulous and hellish the means"; white Texans must do whatever necessary "for the preservation of their independence and the protection of their property."[4] Such sentiments swept the lower South in those weeks and propelled it out of the Union. The outbreak of war provoked even more anxiety about slavery and a fiercer determination to preserve it. "We cannot be too vigilant [in] these perilous times," warned an Atlanta newspaper editor in May 1861. "Our enemies will send incendiaries in disguise among us, who will incite our slave population to deeds of violence and bloodshed."[5] George Womble, a slave in Talbot County, Georgia, heard his master announce that "he was going to join the army and bring Abe Lincoln's head back for a soap dish. He also said that he would wade in blood up to his neck to keep the slaves from being freed."[6]

How blacks would behave in these troubled times was a question much on the minds of whites. Not all agreed with the Atlanta editor that slaves would be susceptible to Yankee incitement. Content with their Biblically sanctioned lot in life and grateful for the paternal care lavished on them, they would spurn the enemy and cleave to their masters—or so some whites asserted. "None of the Southern gentlemen have the smallest apprehension of a servile insurrection," a British traveler in Louisiana remarked in May 1861. "They use the univer[s]al formula 'our negroes are the happiest, most contented, and most comfortable people on the face of the earth.'"[7] An Augusta, Georgia, newspaper editor made a similar boast at about the same time: "[T]here is not a negro in all this land that would not fight to the death if necessary, before he would be torn from the master and mistress of his affection."[8] Free blacks were likewise dependable, in the opinion of some whites; a Savannah newspaper editor, writing in June 1861, commended "their earnest sympathy with our cause."[9]

Such trustfulness was, however, a decidedly minority sentiment. Some expressions of confidence were no doubt sincere, but most were probably nothing more than whistling in the dark or an attempt to prettify the Confederacy in order to influence foreign or domestic opinion of it. The truth is that in the wake of Lincoln's election most Southern whites were deeply fearful about what the blacks might do, and they took extraordinary steps to keep them under control. This fear and its consequences were a central theme of the Confederate experience.[10]

Some whites harbored—or at least expressed—only the concern that slaves would run off to the Yankees. "*[C]onsistency* is a stranger to [the Negro's] nature," opined an Alabamian, "and though he may be faithful, obedient and devoted under the immediate eye of his master, yet few masters can put their fingers on one whom they felt sure no circumstances could cause to desert them."[11] But many more envisioned truly frightening scenarios. Another Alabamian wrote Confederate president Jefferson Davis a few weeks after the war's outbreak to warn against accepting large numbers of army volunteers and thus stripping the home front of able-bodied white men: "We need . . . them to keep the slaves down, and save ourselves from the horrors of insurrection, which may be an incident of the war. . . . If no check is interposed [on enlistment] . . . *anarchy* will prevail and the slaves [will] become our masters, if they can."[12]

In the superheated atmosphere of the months following Lincoln's election, rumors of organized slave insurrections were rife. The Old South was no stranger to such scares (which were almost always false alarms), but now they seemed to be cropping up everywhere, and in many cases they involved an alleged white instigator. Between January and June 1861 there were reports of planned uprisings—in each case discovered and foiled by vigilant whites—in Weston, Virginia; Leonardtown, Maryland; Owen and Gallatin counties, Kentucky; White, Prairie, Randolph, and Monroe counties, Arkansas; St. Martin Parish, Louisiana; Carroll, Adams, Jefferson, and Franklin counties, Mississippi; Decatur County, Georgia; and a number of other places. This wave crested in June, but rumors of uprising plots continued to agitate the minds of whites periodically throughout the war.[13]

The rebellious slaves' intentions, according to reports, ranged from disturbing to nightmarish. Some sought only freedom, but others were bent on vengeance and even lustful gratification. In eastern Arkansas, would-be insurrectionists supposedly intended "to commence a regular wholesale system of murder, plunder and house burning."[14] In Maryland they planned to massacre every white above the age of two.[15] In southwest Georgia they were acquiring guns and meant to "kill all of the [white] men and old women and children and take the younger [women] for their wives."[16]

Deeply alarmed, in many cases panicked, by the specter of black rebellion, whites reacted forcefully. No sooner were the 1860 presidential ballots tallied than the South turned to strengthening its domestic defenses, continuing in a now intensified form a response sparked in 1859, when a Northern abolitionist named John Brown had attempted to incite a slave rebellion in Virginia. The outbreak of war in April 1861 made internal security even more urgent and spurred further protective measures.

State and local governments moved to tighten control of slaves and free blacks. Town councils beefed up their police forces and more rigorously enforced the municipal codes that regulated black behavior. Mississippi's legislature passed a law prohibiting rural slaveowners from quartering their blacks farther than one mile from the master's residence.[17] Maryland forbade blacks to establish any secret society and prescribed harsh punishment for offenders: slaves would receive 39 lashes or be sold away outside the state; free blacks would be fined $50 or more, in default of which they would be sold into temporary slavery; and any free black committing a second such offense would "be sold as a slave for life beyond the limits of the State."[18] Throughout the South, county authorities strengthened their patrols. (The patrol system, a long-established institution in the rural South, required that all white men ride, on a rotating basis, in squads at night through their home district to keep an eye on the black population and especially to apprehend slaves going about without a pass from their owner or holding illicit meetings.)[19]

In many communities during the secession and early war months white men bolstered security and tightened the screws on blacks by enlisting in informal police forces. Known variously as home guards, committees of safety, or vigilance committees, these armed, extralegal bands reinforced or substituted for the legally authorized patrols. In Southampton County, Virginia, for example, men and boys aged 16 to 60 gathered just 15 days after Fort Sumter's surrender and formed a home guard, its task being, as a local resident noted in his diary, to scout around in squads of 9 to 11 men and bring to light "all misconduct of negrows and low life white people of the County and to keep the state of affair[s] right."[20] Citizens of Albemarle County, Virginia, likewise formed a local defense unit, dubbed the Holcomb Guards, soon after the war started; its purpose, as one member wrote, was "to protect our homes[,] to patrol the county[,] and keep the negroes in place."[21]

Whether all these precautions would suffice to suppress black rebelliousness was uncertain. Many whites worried that they would prove inadequate, especially if some disruptive external force made its presence felt. With Yankee armies massing along the Confederacy's borders, the threat of outside interference loomed frighteningly. Even as they scrutinized the black people in their midst, Southern whites nervously scanned the northern horizon.

Within weeks of the attack on Fort Sumter, Union military forces began penetrating Rebel territory. Confederate forces repulsed some of these incursions, but by the late spring of 1862 the Yankees controlled northern Virginia, west and middle Tennessee, northern Alabama, and a number of small enclaves on the Confederate periphery, not to mention almost all sections of the nonseceding Southern states (Missouri, Kentucky, Maryland, and Delaware).[22]

In every part of the South they occupied, Union commanders confronted the question of what to do about slavery. Their response, in those first 15 months or so of the war, was a grim disappointment to the slaves and a pleasant surprise to their masters. The Lincoln administration's policy was thoroughly conservative. Vowing that he intended only to restore the Union, and convinced that threatening slavery would only make the Confederates fight harder for independence and might provoke the nonseceding slave states to reconsider their loyalty, Lincoln ordered his forces to keep their hands off the

South's peculiar institution. Army and navy officers generally obeyed this order, often assuring the citizens of the invaded regions that the North had no radical aims.[23] The general commanding the force that occupied Virginia's eastern shore counties in November 1861 issued a proclamation promising the inhabitants that his troops "will go among you as friends. . . . Special directions have been given not to interfere with the condition of any persons held to domestic service."[24] One of his subordinates had the local folk assemble as soon as the troops marched in and then delivered a conciliatory speech: "Will your negroes be taken away from you? No. If any slaves come inside of the lines, you may search for them. . . . [Y]ou shall have every opportunity to get your negroes back."[25]

This officer, and others like him, were as good as their word. During the war's first months a number of slaves, acting on their faith that the Yankees came as liberators, slipped away from their masters and made their way to the Union army camps. Few, however, got the reception they hoped for. Many were brusquely turned away by sentries. Others were taken in, only to be ejected when an officer discovered their presence or when their master appeared demanding their return. Some of these incidents were heart-rending, rivaling the scenes enacted before the war in Northern cities when slaves who had followed the "underground railroad" to freedom were caught and returned to their masters, courtesy of the federal Fugitive Slave Act. In June 1862, a teenage boy was retrieved from the camp of the 19th Illinois Infantry in Fayetteville, Tennessee; a crowd of soldiers stood by and watched as the master tied the struggling boy to a mule and led him away.[26] Even uglier was the fate of a black man on Virginia's eastern shore in late 1861. After running off to an army camp repeatedly, only to be driven away each time, he finally succeeded in securing shelter there. But then his master came to claim him, and he was promptly turned over—but not before the commanding officer, the same man who had promised the citizens "every opportunity to get your negroes back," had him whipped.[27]

The Lincoln administration did, of course, eventually declare war on slavery, and the Yankee army became the liberating host that the slaves had envisioned (see chapter 4). But it is important to understand that this revolutionary transformation of Union war aims had no direct impact on most slaves until the war was over. Blue-clad armies continued to invade and occupy sections of the Confederacy, but they did not do so for the sake of territorial conquest per se. They did so only where it was useful in achieving their primary goal, which was to destroy the Rebel armies. As late as May 1865 only a small portion of Confederate territory was actually under Union control, and most slaves remained far from a Yankee army post or encampment.[28] Smaller federal forces temporarily penetrated other parts of the Confederacy during the war, but some of these raiding parties declined to act as liberators because the burden of fugitive slaves would slow them down. Moreover, some sections of the Confederacy were exempted from Lincoln's Emancipation Proclamation, as were the nonseceding slave states.

Whether the Yankees were near or far, and whether they were welcoming or not, slaves were hindered from seeking freedom by the rigid restrictions and supervision imposed by the white community and governmental authorities in 1860–61. To these were added the increasingly strict oversight of the slaveowners themselves. Even as masters insisted, as many did, that their own slaves were perfectly content and loyal (it was all the other slaves they were worried about, they said), they began watching them more closely. Some grew stingier in issuing the passes that allowed their slaves to leave home on Sundays to visit with others in the neighborhood or to stay overnight with a spouse owned by a different master. Many began to take special precautions around Christmas, traditionally a time when work was suspended, rules were relaxed, and joyous celebrations were held in the slave quarters.[29]

Not content with stricter supervision, many masters also tried persuasion. They reminded their slaves that the benevolent care they received should be repaid with obedience and loyalty. One concerned plantation lady began in 1862 a program of regular Bible readings to the black folk, no doubt emphasizing passages such as Colossians 3:22. Many tried to deter potential fugitives by spreading horror stories about the Yankees. The enemy has come not to free the slaves, masters said, but to ravage the South and abuse its inhabitants, black and white alike. If the brutal minions of the North did not simply murder the slaves outright—which some masters swore they would do—they would yoke them like oxen and put them to hauling wagons. Another story told by slaveowners had the Yankees transporting all the slaves who fell into their hands to Cuba and selling them.[30] One plantation owner, who in late 1863 visited a federal post in Mississippi where runaways congregated, subsequently called his own slaves together and gave a graphic account of what he had seen: "all kinds of suffering, . . . the graves of negroes, . . . acres of the most miserable little huts [in which the blacks lived] . . . not a morsel of salt and but little meat, all the able bodied negro men were put in the army, the others were left to shift for themselves."[31]

When enemy raiding parties approached, masters did not rely on persuasion alone to keep their slaves from running off. Many quickly mustered their black people, marched them away to a hiding place, and kept them there until the alarm was over. Some prepared well in advance for such emergencies, readying a secluded spot and stockpiling provisions.[32] When Yankee armies invaded and permanent occupation of the area seemed likely, masters often took more drastic measures, gathering up their slaves and as many other personal possessions as they could haul, abandoning their homes, moving to a safe place in the Confederate interior, and reestablishing themselves there. Many tens of thousands of black people were thus turned into refugees during the war in order to keep them enslaved (see chapter 3).

As the war continued, masters and the white community as a whole made it known with increasing vehemence that slave disloyalty would not be tolerated. In October 1862 citizens of Hempstead, Texas, held a public meeting at which they formally resolved to ask the state legislature "to enact a law making it a capital crime for any slave to desert from his master with the intent of going over to the enemy." Anticipating the passage of such legislation, they appointed from among themselves an executive committee whose responsibilities would include "try[ing] and hang[ing] any negro caught in attempting to escape to the enemy."[33] The white community spoke with actions as well as words. The home guards formed in 1861 remained on duty, in many cases, throughout the war years, and new ones were sometimes organized where trouble threatened. Plagued by Yankee raids and restless slaves, a hundred citizens of King and Queen County, Virginia, met in the village of Providence in June 1863 and formed themselves into a home guard. "[T]here was great unanimity of sentiment," one attendee reported; the citizens were "aroused to the necessity of home defense to protect themselves and property."[34]

The measures enacted by state and local governments in 1860–61 to preserve slavery were reinforced by others as the war went on, often in response to enemy invasions. In late December 1861, following the capture of Port Royal and other islands off the South Carolina coast by a Union amphibious force, that state's legislature passed *An Act to provide more efficient Police Regulations for the Districts on the Sea-board* (districts being the equivalent of counties in that state). It mandated that in each of the five coastal districts (where huge rice and cotton plantations dominated the landscape and slaves greatly outnumbered whites) a five-man Police Court be established. These courts would have "full power in regard to slaves and free persons of color," instituting whatever regulations and imposing whatever punishments they deemed necessary; their decrees would supersede all existing black codes and be "final and without appeal."[35] A year later, with the enemy in greater strength on the islands and threatening to invade the mainland, South Carolina's governor mobilized the state militia, which embraced every white male ages 16 to 65. Militia officers were "to organize, drill and arm the [precinct] companies in every district, and have them ready to act as a police force." Invoking the specter of Yankee-incited "disturbance amongst our slaves or resistance to their masters," the governor declared that "we owe it to our families and to the country to be active and guarded. . . . Let every man sleep by his arms."[36]

Following the capture of New Orleans by Union forces in April 1862, many of Louisiana's southeastern parishes enacted more stringent slave-control measures. St. Landry Parish thoroughly reorganized its patrol system; the superintendent of patrols was ordered to see that patrol districts were delineated, a captain appointed for each, records kept, reports rendered, and every white male from 16 to 60 enrolled and put to work.[37] West Baton Rouge Parish, on the Mississippi River upstream from New Orleans, likewise took action. Citing "the exigencies of the times," the parish authorities created a standing committee to advise the police chief on security measures, directed the chief to hire a special guard of 20 men to patrol the parish at night, ordered him to post 4 men armed with double-barreled shotguns in skiffs on the river "to prevent . . . the absconding of the slave population," and authorized him to seize and secure in a safe place all the small boats in the parish "as a precautionary measure to prevent the escape of slaves."[38] In St. Charles Parish, also upriver from New Orleans but even closer to it, the authorities convened an emergency "Extra Sitting" in May 1862 to amend the slave-patrol ordinance they had enacted in December 1860. Not only did they now reorganize the patrol, they also created a separate "River Police" whose duty was "to keep a night and day watch on the bank of [the] river and also on the river in boats, and to arrest all negroes passing up or down in skiffs or otherwise."[39]

However vigilant they were, home-guard, militia, patrol, and river-police forces were weakened by military enlistment and conscription. The Confederate government began conscription in April 1862; as later amended, the law made all able-bodied white men ages 17 to 50, with certain exceptions, liable for military service. Between volunteers and draftees, Southern communities were stripped of white men. Nevertheless, the institutions of slave control survived in most localities until the war's end. They did so by drawing more and more on teenage boys, older men, draft-exempt men such as plantation overseers, and men of military age physically unfit for army duty but still able to ride a horse and carry a gun. Georgia's legislature responded to the home-front manpower shortage by raising the upper age limit of men required to do patrol duty from 45 to 60. In many places boys as young as 16 had to ride patrol, and even younger ones did so voluntarily.[40]

The civilian manpower shortage was offset in part, too, by the Confederate army's growing role in preserving slavery. The military became in fact a key agent of that vital endeavor. Army officers often took steps to keep slaves in their localities orderly and to capture runaways, and they cooperated closely with slaveowners and civil authorities in doing so. A general commanding a military district on the South Carolina coast informed one of his subordinates in 1862 that slave control was his primary task: "You will locate your troops with a view to prevent the escape of slaves and for protection of persons and property against insubordination of negroes."[41] Mounted Rebel outfits in Mississippi—at least one of which actually began life as a county slave patrol and was later absorbed intact into the army—routinely kept an eye out for fugitive slaves as they scouted Yankee positions.[42] In northeastern Florida, four cavalry companies and three smaller detachments were posted at strategic points not only to serve as lookouts but also, as their commander reported, to "prevent negroes from escaping to the enemy."[43]

Rebel forces not only watched for runaways but also intervened to prevent escapes and trouble of other sorts. A planter on the South Carolina coast, alerted in 1862 to a planned mass escape by his slaves, called on a nearby Confederate unit for aid; its commander immediately dispatched troops to quell the plot.[44] One day in June 1863, at a Louisiana plantation that lay very close to the Union lines and where the slaves had grown restless and disobedient, a detachment of 25 Confederate soldiers suddenly appeared and, as the plantation owner recorded in his diary, "took away 4 Men and 3 Women by force saying they were dangerous Negros."[45]

In 1862 the Confederate Congress formalized the role of the army in preserving slavery. A law passed in October of that year, implemented by a War Department directive five months later, decreed that runaways captured by troops were to be returned promptly to their owners. If that was infeasible, they were to be sent under guard to a special holding depot, 19 of which were to be set up in various locations throughout the Confederacy. Advertisements describing these slaves were to be published in newspapers so their masters could identify and retrieve them. While in army custody, the blacks could be put to work on public projects.[46]

The vast web arrayed by Southern slaveowners, communities, civil authorities, and military commanders snared many thousands of fugitives. In the Albemarle Sound region of coastal North Carolina, where the Union army had gained a foothold on the mainland, security measures were quite successful; one slaveowner there, referring to the local patrols or home guards or both, wrote that "they have organized a very stringent guard on the sound & rivers on both sides of the Sound & they take [i.e., recapture] nearly every [slave] that leaves [his or her master] now."[47] Sharp-eyed Confederate scouts intercepted many runaways on their way to the Union lines. A cavalry battalion commander in northern Mississippi wrote his superior in January 1863 (before the War Department issued its directive on the matter) asking what to do with the would-be escapees his troopers were gathering in who refused to reveal their master's name and place of residence; "the number," he remarked, "is increasing beyond convenience."[48]

Often, alert citizens acting on their own foiled escape attempts. One night in October 1863 20 slaves slipped away from the city of Savannah in a boat and headed down the Savannah River toward the Yankee garrison at Fort Pulaski on the seacoast. The boat capsized, however, drowning some of the fugitives; those who made it to shore were promptly rounded up by a white man who lived nearby and had a pack of bloodhounds at his disposal. Just four nights later another band of slaves, these from a plantation above the city, stole two boats and likewise attempted to follow the river to Fort Pulaski; but they were spotted at daybreak by a riverboat captain and his crew, who headed them off and forced their surrender. Sometimes slaveowners needed no assistance in retrieving runaways. Told one day in May 1863 that they were about to be moved to another state far away, 14 slaves in northern Mississippi deserted their plantation that night, heading for the Union lines in west Tennessee. Their master tracked down 9 of them with dogs the very next day, and on the following day led them off toward their new home, 2 of them in chains.[49]

Fugitives such as these, who lived on the periphery of Confederate territory, within striking distance of Union lines, clearly faced enormous odds, but they had at least a chance of success, however slight. Slaves who tried to escape from deeper inside

Rebeldom had virtually no chance, for it was nearly impossible to avoid every one of the myriad dangers over a long distance. The travail of Wallace Turnage, a slave on a cotton plantation in west-central Alabama, is illustrative. In June 1861, unable any longer to endure the brutality of his overseer, Turnage fled the plantation. Cautiously making his way northward, keeping mostly to the woods and avoiding white people, he was making good progress when he unexpectedly encountered an elderly white man who was out hunting. "[W]ho do you belong to boy[?]" the man demanded, and followed that with an order to halt. Turnage jumped into some thick bushes and ran, as shotgun pellets tore through the leaves all around him. Continuing his flight, he made the mistake of stepping out of the woods onto a road where it ran by a house. Again he was accosted by a suspicious white man, who demanded to see his pass. Again Turnage ran, chased by the man's dogs, and once more he got away. But his flight ended some time later when he was spotted by yet another wary white man; this one pulled a pistol, got the drop on Turnage, and returned him to his owner. Through it all, Turnage never got farther than 27 miles from home. Twice more, in the fall of 1861 and the fall of 1862, he fled the plantation and headed north. Both times he was caught and taken back to his master. The third attempt ended when he fell into the clutches of some Rebel troops.[50]

Even in the war's last months, by which time conscription and volunteering had badly depleted home-front manpower and casualties had taken a terrible toll on the army, the web of enforcement continued, in most parts of the Confederacy, to entangle many a fugitive. In September 1864 several dozen Mississippi slaves banded together, stole horses, and set out toward Natchez, which was held by the Union army. None of them made it there: 15 miles from the city they were intercepted by a detachment of Rebel cavalry. Slaves in the besieged Confederate capital of Richmond were continually thwarted in their escape attempts, despite the proximity of the Yankee lines. There, in addition to all the other hazards that runaways faced, a municipal detective force was on duty with orders to guard against escape attempts. Among the many slaves whose hopes were dashed by alert detectives were six women and five men who tried to get away along the Darbytown Road one night in February 1865. Of course, even if they had eluded the detectives they would have had to slip by suspicious white citizens and watchful Confederate pickets before they got to the Union lines. In any event, by the time the sun rose all 11 were locked up in the city's Castle Thunder prison awaiting their masters' arrival.[51]

Nor were the agents and institutions of slavery enforcement at work solely in Confederate territory. Until late in the war they were active also in the nonseceding slave states. Although occupied by the Union army, these states were not under military rule; civil authority persisted there, and the Emancipation Proclamation did not apply. The experience of two eastern Kentucky slaves named Peter and Phil in the summer of 1863 is a case in point. Having run away with the aim of getting across the Ohio River to the free states, the two made it only 50 miles or so. In a village well south of the river they were nabbed by a small band of armed white men. These men took the slaves to a nearby building and held them overnight, bound with ropes. "They . . . told us they were Nigger Catchers and that was the way they made their living," Peter later recounted; they had only to look at a black person, they boasted, to know if he or she was a run-away. In the morning the men handcuffed Peter and Phil and took them to the county seat of Flemingsburg, where, following long-established procedure regarding recap-tured fugitives, they went before a magistrate and swore that the two blacks were run-aways. After being forced to reveal their owners' names and residences, Peter and Phil were lodged in the county jail. There they remained while the authorities notified their owners. After two weeks an agent employed by the owners appeared, paid the jail ex-penses and slave-catchers' fee as required by law, and took the two men home. Reading Peter's account, one might easily mistake this for an antebellum episode, so devoid is it of any evidence that the war that had been raging for more than two years had dis-turbed the institution of slavery.[52]

The network of vigilance, precautions, and regulations in place inside and outside the Confederacy not only ensnared thousands of black freedom-seekers and returned them to bondage, it also discouraged untold numbers of other slaves from even trying to escape. In a letter to President Davis in November 1863 an official of the Duplin County court in eastern North Carolina took note of the deterrent effect of strong se-curity measures. Praising the county patrol—which had been equipped with a pack of bloodhounds purchased with money voluntarily contributed by the citizenry—he informed the president that it was "of *great* service in preventing escapes of Slaves. . . . We are here not far distant from the Yankee lines; and you well Know a good watch should be Kept. Since the organization of this Company, there has been *no* attempt of escapes by the Slaves *but one* (save in the [Yankee] Raid in July)."[53]

Whites deterred potential runaways not only by making a strong show of force and by recapturing many slaves who did run, but also by punishing—often brutally—those who were recaptured. The whip was the instrument of choice for correcting errant blacks in the war years, as in the antebellum years; other devices were employed as needed. Two women caught after running off from an eastern North Carolina planta-tion in 1863 suffered the wrath of an overseer named Bateman, whose temper was so fierce it worried even one of his white neighbors. "My only fear (between ourselves)," the neighbor confided in a letter to the absent owner of the slaves, "is that Bateman will be too severe with those negroes, for . . . he seemed very angry with them & he said he al-ready struck one two hundred [times]."[54] Slaves at Oak Lawn plantation on the South Carolina coast whose 1862 escape attempt was foiled were taught a lesson by their mas-ter. As he explained in a letter, he "proceeded to punish them by whips and handcuff-ing. Sam and Thomas [have been] sent to the Work House in Charleston to be sold." Even those Oak Lawn slaves not involved in the attempt suffered for it: they were "being watched and chained at night until the police of the river can be secured [so] as to leave us at liberty to release them."[55]

After being claimed by his owner's agent in Flemingsburg, the Kentucky fugitive Peter endured cruelties that were still vivid in his mind when he wrote his memoir decades later:

> The next morning when John Cockrel came in the jail after us he whipped Phil and myself both with a cowhide before he took us out of the jail. Then he took out of his saddle bag a large new chain and two locks. He then locked one end of the chain around Phil's neck and the other around my neck and then we were locked together. Then he took our shoes off and put them into his saddle bag and he said that he intended to wear all of the skin off of our feet before we reached home. . . .
>
> Every few hundred yards he would whip us that cruel way until we had reached our destination. Whenever he would have to stop over night he would just lock us up in a bare room with no bed to sleep on or chairs to sit on, and he told the people where we stopped, that he did not care whether we had anything to eat or not and all the time we were in there Phil and myself were still locked together. He never unlocked us. . . .
>
> At last we reached Irvin[e] and he took us on by home and put us in jail. . . . My master came in jail that evening and asked me what did I think ought to be done with me and I told him I did not care what he did with me. So he had a blacksmith to come in that evening and take the measure around my neck, he intended to have an iron yoke made to go around my neck, and extend out about eighteen inches, then extend up sixteen inches, and he was going to have a bell fastened to that so whenever I ran away he could hear the bell ringing, and by that way I would not be able to get very far before they would catch me. . . .
>
> The next morning my master came in, drunk as usual. I told him if he put that yoke on me I would jump into the river and drown myself. So then he took me up to the blacksmith's and had him make a hobble to fit my ankle and had a new trace chain run through it and riveted it around my leg. Then he had a long staple made to drive into the wall to lock me up to every night. Then they led me all over town just similar to a chained bear; they led me around to show me. . . . [A white farmer who hired Peter from his master] took me home that evening and drove the staple in the wall and chained me up. My master told him to whip me every day if it was necessary, to whip me until he was satisfied, it did not make any difference if he killed me.[56]

Some recaptured runaways did in fact suffer death, at the hands of their masters or other whites. Sometimes this ultimate penalty was inflicted in anger, sometimes coolly, even ceremoniously. A Florida slave named Gus was hanged by the Rebel soldiers who caught him heading for the Union lines in 1862. A Missourian named Alfred did not survive long after running away from his master in October 1863: he was apprehended by a gang of whites who took him back home, whipped him, and then—reportedly at the urging of the master's infuriated wife, who offered $5 for the deed—put a pistol bullet through his heart. Most of the several dozen mounted fugitives intercepted by Confederate cavalry on their way to Natchez in 1864 were gunned down rather than taken prisoner. A few masters, mostly large slaveholders who deemed the sacrifice of a valuable bondsman a reasonable price to pay for a good deterrent, had recaptured runaways executed in the presence of other slaves.[57] One was a Mississippi planter named Wallace who ordered two of his slaves to be thus hanged and then invited his neighbors to bring their own slaves over for a look. Louis Hughes, one of those forced to attend this grisly exhibit, wrote of it in his memoir: "I shall never forget the horror of the scene—it was sickening. The bodies hung at the roadside . . . until the blue flies literally swarmed around them, and the stench was fearful."[58]

Recaptured fugitives were not the only blacks who suffered deadly retribution in the wartime South. In the volatile atmosphere of suspicion and fear that pervaded the region, any act of black perfidy, self-assertion, aggression, resistance, or conspiracy—whether real or imagined—could provoke a murderous response. Mob violence against black transgressors, not unknown in the antebellum era, proliferated after Lincoln's election and especially after the outbreak of war. The orgy of lynching that marked the late 19th- and early 20th-century South had a predecessor in the Civil War.

The mobs acted in some cases in the heat of passion, in other cases deliberately, with a show of due procedure. The victims included women as well as men. When fire destroyed a house and damaged a store and warehouse in the southern Mississippi town of Osyka on March 19, 1864, two slaves named Mary and Tina found themselves accused of arson. They confessed, no doubt encouraged by the lash, and further admitted that they had planned also to murder their masters' families and then flee to the Yankees. Their masters, too impatient to let the law take its course, "turned said slaves over to the good people of the County," as they explained in a petition to the state legislature, "by whom after thorough and dispassionate investigation, they were duly executed by hanging."[59]

George, a slave in Harris County, Georgia, accused in February 1861 of breaking into a house and assaulting a white woman, seemed at first to have the benefit of legal process. A justice of the peace examined the case, found sufficient cause to proceed with prosecution, and committed George to jail to await the April term of the Superior Court. Four days later, however, a mob gathered outside the jail demanding summary punishment. The local newspaper described what followed: "They rushed to the jail, and . . . with axe, hammer and crowbar, violently broke through the doors and took the prisoner out, carrying him about two miles from town, where they chained him to a tree and *burned him* to death. . . . [T]he negro protested his innocence with his last breath."[60]

The list of such incidents is long; so too the roll of victims. In May 1861 a self-appointed citizens' committee in Arkansas hanged three black men and a white man for plotting insurrection. That same month, a slave in Georgia suspected of the same crime suffered the same fate. In July five Alabama blacks were burned to death for murdering their overseer. Two months later an Arkansas slave was lynched for stabbing an overseer and a Maryland slave for attempting to rape a white girl. In the spring of 1862 five Alabama slaves were put to death by a citizens' committee for the murder of their master; the two who carried out the killing suffered death by burning, and the three who disposed of the body were hanged. In September an east Tennessee slave supposedly involved in the murder of his master was seized by neighbors, who hanged him on the spot. A Maryland slave named as the father by a pregnant, 17-year-old white girl in April 1863 likewise died at the end of rope without benefit of trial. Five months later an Atlanta slave in jail on a charge of insulting a white woman was taken by a mob and hanged. In July 1864 Confederate soldiers in Mississippi seized from the civil authorities a black man accused of assaulting a white woman and hanged him from a tree limb. In Georgia the following month a citizens' committee tried and executed a white man and three blacks for attempted insurrection. The extralegal slaughter reached a horrific apogee in the fall of 1861, when 40 or more black men in the Natchez area, having endured interrogation under torture by citizens who had gotten wind of an insurrection plot, died by hanging.[61]

Some whites condemned these lynchings. The editor of the Harris County, Georgia, newspaper that reported the murder of George entered a "solemn protest" against it: "We are opposed to mobs in every shape," he declared—but then added, "except in cases where there is imminent danger to be apprehended by delay."[62] Other whites agreed that "imminent danger" justified circumventing the law; unlike the editor, however, most regarded such danger as inherent and ubiquitous in these turbulent times. Answering the editor's criticism of the lynching, an assemblage of Harris County citizens met three days after its publication and formally resolved that "We feel ourselves right in the sight of God and the world, in committing the deed."[63] The Osyka, Mississippi, masters who handed their black women over to the citizenry for punishment defended their action; it was, they said, a justifiable response to the "insurrectionary and barbarous" intentions of these "extremely dangerous" slaves. So convinced were they of the propriety of their course that they asked the state to reimburse them for the value of the women as it would have been obliged to do "had said slaves been executed by due process of law."[64] A letter printed in a Mississippi newspaper, reporting the 1864 incident of the Confederate soldiers who seized and hanged the slave accused of attempted rape, offered this rationale for the lynching: "In such cases, and in such times, the ceremony of law is a farce."[65]

The reign of racial terror in the wartime South, and the network of vigilance that bolstered it, served their purpose well. Many slaves who dreamed of escape reluctantly concluded that the risk was too great and resigned themselves to continued servitude.

There were other slaves, however—a minority, to be sure, but a significant minority—who chose not to seek freedom for reasons besides fear of retribution.

Some were persuaded that what the Yankees offered was no improvement over slavery. The stories masters spread about the awful fate of blacks in the enemy's hands, while privately scoffed at by many slaves, convinced others. "I wus afraid of de Yankees," North Carolinian Andrew Boone recalled many years after the war, "'cause de [whites] had told us dat de Yankees would kill us. Dey tole us dat de Yankees would bore holes in our shoulders an' wurk us to carts. Dey tole us we would be treated a lot worser den dey wus treating us."[66] The slaves' enforced ignorance was a factor here; most were not just illiterate in the narrow sense but more generally unknowledgeable about the world beyond their immediate surroundings, and thus in some ways manipulable. Very young slaves, who like all children were innocent and impressionable, less able than their elders to distinguish truth from fabrication, were especially vulnerable to such scare-mongering.[67]

Other slaves were convinced of the Yankees' malevolence not by rumor or propaganda but by credible testimony or firsthand experience. A Tennessean who fled to the camps soon after Union troops arrived in March 1862 returned the very next day, reporting (as his owner's daughter noted in her diary) that the soldiers had "put him to hard work—about noon they gave him a pail to get some water, he gave them the slip and came home . . . says he will never leave his master again."[68] (This slave, like some others, was apparently confident that in returning voluntarily he would be spared the punishment so often inflicted on those who were returned unwillingly.) A white North Carolinian told what happened after a slave named Jim deserted his plantation and took refuge in the Union-held town of Plymouth: he "stayed a few weeks then ran away from the Yankees and returned . . . says [he] has had enough of the Yankees, they made him work very hard and fed him badly. Mr. Spruill [the overseer] says the other negroes behave much better since Jim's return."[69] Prince, a Louisiana slave, explained to a white man in 1863 why he was anxious to avoid falling into the enemy's hands: "[T]hese black folks that come back [from the Union lines] say the Yankees takes all the young looking fellows and puts them in the army, and I've no notion of going in the army."[70] Sometimes fearful slaves hid out to avoid Union troops or refused to go off with those they encountered who offered to free them. Many younger slave women were particularly afraid of Northern soldiers because of the threat of rape—a form of racial abuse not unknown in the invaded regions.[71]

Forces of attraction rather than repulsion kept some slaves from going to the Yankees. There were those who were treated well enough by their master and content enough with their other circumstances that slavery seemed no affliction and freedom offered no enticement. In certain cases a strong emotional bond kept the slave loyal to the master; in other cases it was the slave's sense of having a personal stake in maintaining the home that the two shared. These impulses were most common among slaves whose circumstances fostered interracial intimacy, especially those who lived on farms rather than plantations and those on plantations whose work kept them in the Big House close to their owners rather than in the fields, such as manservants, maidservants, and mammies.[72]

A man named Burrel, who lived on a 160-acre farm in northeastern Florida with his owner's family and eight or nine other slaves, embodied both impulses. While his master, Winston Stephens, was away in the Confederate army Burrel assumed management of the farm. "Tell Burrel . . . I shall trust to his care every thing," Winston wrote to his wife, Octavia, in 1863, "knowing he feels an interest in what I have." Winston's trust was not misplaced. Burrel faithfully tended the crops, saw to the welfare of the other slaves (one of whom was his wife and four his children), and sent Winston regular reports on farm matters by way of letters written by Octavia, who was utterly dependent on him to keep the place going. The letters conveyed not only Burrel's commitment to the farm but also his affection for his master: "Burrel sends [a] 'heap of howdies' to you," Octavia wrote on one occasion. The presence of Union troops in the area offered Burrel any number of chances to flee, but he spurned them.[73]

A more general attachment to community led some slaves to reject freedom. Black people in the Old South, no less than whites, were deeply imbedded in communities that provided fellowship, encouragement, mutual aid, and spiritual nourishment. These communities were sustained by the camaraderie of the slave quarters, by the custom of Sunday visiting among slaves on neighboring farms and plantations, and by the churches that many blacks joined. To flee to the Yankees meant leaving not just a master but friends and kinfolk and Christian brethren, not just a household but one's little place in the world. Such a wrenching departure could not be undertaken lightly, for it might mean cutting ties forever.[74]

In some cases the black community discouraged desertion. The Mattaponi Baptist Church of King and Queen County, Virginia, provides an example. Like nearly all other rural churches in the South in that era it was biracial, embracing both the white and black faithful, and while controlled by the whites it allowed the blacks a measure of self-governance. On August 9, 1862, the blacks exercised that power, as the church secretary recorded in his minute book: "[T]he coloured members in full meeting . . . excommunicated from their fellowship the following persons for having left the service of their owners and gone off to the yankees[,] an enemy with whom the southern confederacy is at war." A list of 21 names was appended.[75]

It may be, of course, that this excommunication represented not the sentiments of Mattaponi's black members but the demands of its white members. There are, in historical records, many avowals of black loyalty that sound suspiciously like a white person being told what he or she wanted to hear by a slave long accustomed to the necessity of deception. And yet others are recorded that are clearly genuine. A woman named Emily, a slave on a Louisiana plantation, was one of those who, like Burrel, rejected freedom and remained contentedly at home without compulsion. Her overseer gave this report of her behavior during a Yankee raid in 1863: "[O]ne of the officers tolde her that he wolde take her a longe & set her free [but] she told him that she was as near free as she wist to be & had a good home & was goinge to stay at it."[76]

Whether numbered among the few like Emily and Burrel who refused to leave their masters or the many who longed for freedom but were denied it, most slaves in the wartime South remained in bondage. They toiled away, as they always had, for the profit and comfort of white people. This did not mean, however, that they were altogether untouched by the war. On farms and plantations, in villages, towns, and cities, the enslaved were swept up in the great struggle being waged over the South's future, and their own.

Two

LIFE AND LABOR ON THE LAND

Mid-19th-century black Southerners were tillers of the soil. The great majority of slaves worked in agriculture, most on plantations with 20 or more black hands, some on farms with only a few. On the farms they labored directly under their master's supervision, often side by side with him in the fields, and lived in a room of his house or in a cabin or lean-to or loft close by. On the plantations they labored in field gangs (unless assigned to other duty) under a white overseer employed by the master or a black "driver" owned by him, and they lived in the cluster of cabins called the slave quarters some distance from the Big House. Most free blacks in the South also lived in the countryside; many hired out as farm hands and a few owned farms of their own.

Enslaved field hands grew the crops and tended the livestock that not only put money in their master's pocket but also fed him and his family and themselves. Corn, pork, garden vegetables, and dairy products provided the bulk of the nourishment for blacks and whites alike in the Old South. Hands divided their time between producing food and producing the crops that their master sold for profit. These crops varied by region. Short-staple cotton was the most widespread and most important; it could be raised everywhere in the South save the Border states and Appalachian highlands, where the growing season was too short. Tobacco and wheat were grown in the Border and other Upper South states, sugarcane in southern Louisiana, and rice and long-staple cotton in the lowcountry and offshore islands of South Carolina, Georgia, and northeastern Florida.

The rhythm of life on farms and plantations was dictated by the cycle of the seasons and the demands of the crops. Each crop made distinctive demands and imposed its own calendar of planting, cultivating, and harvesting, but what most slaves learned were the routines of corn culture and short-staple cotton culture, which pretty much coincided. In late winter or early spring, field hands harnessed mules or oxen to plows and prepared for planting by breaking and furrowing the fields. Once the cotton and corn seeds had been sowed and were sprouting, the workers took up hoes. After months of hoeing to thin out the growing plants and eliminate weeds and more plowing to keep the soil loosened up, the plants were able to survive on their own and needed no further cultivation. Thus began, in the late summer, what was called the laying-by time, a respite when the hands could relax. This was followed by several weeks of intense activity in the fall, when the ripe cotton bolls and corn ears had to be hurriedly picked before they spoiled. Harvest time was succeeded by the less hectic months of late fall and winter, but even those were busy with the myriad other chores of agricultural life: slaughtering hogs, preserving the meat, feeding livestock, mending fences, repairing buildings, cutting firewood, and on and on.

Slaves on farms and plantations usually worked from sunrise to sunset—"from can't-see to can't-see," as they said—in all seasons. Six days of work a week was the rule, although some masters gave a half day off on Saturday along with the obligatory day of rest on Sunday. Much of this labor was gender- or age-specific. While both men and women hoed the crops, the heavy work of plowing was almost always done by men. Women tended vegetable gardens, either a small one for their own family or a large communal one. On the biggest plantations, where greater division of labor was possible, some slaves worked as skilled artisans—coopers, blacksmiths, carpenters, and so forth; these were all men. Women exercised their skills in textile production with spinning wheel and loom. Some slaves served the master and his family personally: women as cooks, laundresses, or maids; men as butlers, manservants, or carriage drivers. Slave children, except for the very young, had their chores, too: feeding chickens, milking cows, and fetching water. Very old slaves were generally excused from work, although some elderly women were assigned daycare duty with babies and younger children to free the mothers to work in the fields or Big House.[1]

The outbreak of war propelled a tidal wave through Southern society but only a ripple through agricultural routine. Masters were determined that work would continue on their farms and plantations despite the commotion in the world outside. David Golightly Harris's farm in the South Carolina piedmont, with 10 slaves, 100 cultivated acres, and 450 acres of woodland, provides an example of such continuity amid turbulence.

"War & Rumors of wars," Harris exclaimed in his diary on April 12, 1861. "Great excitement prevails at this time, on account of a report that Fort Sumter is to be bombarded immediately." That afternoon he went to the nearby village of Spartanburg to learn more, leaving his slaves (three women named Ann, Manerva, and Maria; three men named Elifus, Will, and Edom; a boy named York; and three little children) to go on with the plowing and other tasks unsupervised. After staying overnight in the village and learning that firing had indeed erupted in Charleston harbor, Harris came home to find that "my hands had not done much work in my absence." The excitement continued in the days that followed. Young men of the neighborhood flocked to the colors, boarded trains, and went off to reinforce the Confederate troops at Charleston. Harris made repeated trips to Spartanburg for news, but he also made sure his hands got their work done. Sunday the 14th was of course a day of rest, but on Monday Harris wrote, "The morning pleasant & the land in working order. . . . Will is prepairing a water melon pach in the potatoe lot near the fish-pon." Plowing was halted by rain later that day and prevented by wet soil on Tuesday but resumed on Wednesday. By then Harris had learned that Fort Sumter's garrison had surrendered and that "Pres A Lincoln has issued orders for 75,000 men to Keep the peace &c. This begins to look a little squally." On the 18th he had 10 bushels of shelled corn from the previous year's crop transported to a mill for grinding, but not without some yelling at the slaves to get them cracking on it. Over the next few days the hands did more plowing. By the 22nd Harris could report "The land in good condition for work. . . . [W]ell broken with my new plows, close & deep." That same day, one of the black children performed her inaugural chore: "[O]ur little negro brought her first bucket of water from the spring. That was the first of many trips if she lives long." Corn planting followed the breaking and furrowing of the soil. By the 24th, war news had ceased to dominate Harris's diary. He observed that "Everything is going on as well as could be expected. To day Will has replowed the garden, and it is now ready for planting cabbage." The next day Edom and Elifus set to work clearing out a clogged drainage ditch. As war preparations consumed the outside world, the black people on the Harris farm labored on as they always had.[2]

The familiar cycles of work continued in the Southern countryside as the seasons and years succeeded one another after the spring of 1861. "Sometimes you didn't knowed [the war] was goin' on," recalled former slave Felix Haywood about his youth on a Texas cattle and sheep ranch. "The ranch went on jus' like it always had before the war."[3] Alfred Sligh had a similar memory of the war years on a South Carolina plantation: "Sho' we hear[d] dat all Negroes am free in 1863, but dat rumor [did] not affect us. We work[ed] on."[4] But of course no place, and no person, remained wholly untouched, for the conflict mushroomed into an immense, omnipresent, irresistible, and transforming force. Before long, as another former slave put it, the war came "ter de great house an' ter de slave cabins jist alike."[5]

After the 1861 harvest, many farmers and planters in the Confederacy expanded food production and cut back on nonfood production. They did so at the urging of the Confederate government and often at the command of their state government. A law passed in Arkansas in March 1862, for example, limited growers to two acres of cotton per field hand. Virginia's legislature forbade any planter to raise more than 2,500 tobacco plants per field hand, with a maximum of 80,000 per plantation. Nine of the 11 Confederate states eventually limited nonfood agricultural production in some way. The purpose was, of course, to ensure sufficient food for the Rebel army, many of whose soldiers had left farm work for military service, thus reducing the white labor force available to grow food.[6]

Growing less cotton and tobacco and more corn and wheat altered the work routines of many Southern blacks. Cotton and tobacco were highly labor-intensive crops, corn and wheat much less so. An average field hand could, for example, work as many as 30 acres of corn in a given year but only 8 acres of cotton. The switch to corn and wheat might therefore have meant less work for the hands, had masters not responded by expanding cultivated acreage and taking other steps to keep their workers busy during the growing season. Increased corn production also added to the field hands' burden of stripping corn-plant leaves for use as fodder, a chore that preceded the picking of the ripe ears; it meant, too, more work shucking and shelling after the harvest. Increased wheat crops imposed their own postharvest burden in the form of added threshing. On the other hand, agricultural workers had to spend less time during the war on the laborious processes of cleaning and ginning picked cotton and drying and stripping harvested tobacco.[7]

Overall, the typical black field hand probably worked even harder during the war than before. This was mainly because of the labor shortage that afflicted farms and plantations alike. On the farms, where blacks and whites worked side by side in the fields, the departure of the master's sons (and in many cases the master himself) for the army threw a sizeable extra burden on those who remained at home. The Confederate army's impressment of slaves to work on fortifications (discussed in chapter 3) likewise drained away considerable labor—in this case from farms and plantations both—and the difference had to be made up by those (mostly women) not subject to impressment.

Many rural slaves not assigned to the fields also found that the work demanded of them changed and expanded during the war. In addition to his usual tasks as the plantation blacksmith—shoeing horses and mules, mending broken hoe blades, and so on—Calvin Moye of Rural Shade, Texas, hammered out sabers to equip Confederate cavalrymen.[8] Thomas Jefferson of South Carolina, whose master operated a grain mill along with a plantation and put Jefferson to work as a miller, was also kept busy by the demands of the war effort. "I remember one time," he told an interviewer years afterward, "we worked all night Saturday night, all day Sunday and Sunday night, and [by] Monday morning had ten barrels of flour to send the Confederate army."[9]

As the war continued, many rural slaves also experienced changes in the management of their farm or plantation, for the manpower demands of the Rebel army took away slaveowners and overseers by the tens of thousands. Among these were the 50 slaves on Jack Haley's cotton plantation in Williamson County, Texas. Haley, who had always acted as his own overseer, enlisted soon after the war began, leaving his son John in charge of the place. To assist John, Jack hired an overseer named Delbridge. When conscription took John away sometime later, Delbridge assumed full responsibility for the place. Slaves on the William Harris plantation in Russell County, Alabama, had an experience of the opposite sort: their master had always hired an overseer, but when that man joined the army Harris took over the duties himself.[10]

Because the Confederate conscription law generally allowed an exemption for one man of military age on each place with 20 or more slaves (eventually extended to 15 or more), most of the larger places continued to be managed by a white man.[11] Many small places, however, and some plantations, were left in the hands of a white woman. The enlistment of Ned Cotton in 1861 left his 15-year-old son as the only white male on his Orange County, North Carolina, plantation. No hired overseer stepped in, however, for Cotton's older daughter, known to the slaves as Miss Riah, rose to the occasion. As a former slave on the place recalled, Miss Riah managed the plantation and the laborers "same as a man," overseeing the field gang on horseback and ensuring the continued production of corn, potatoes, and cotton.[12] Less confident, and ultimately less successful, was Emily Harris, wife of David Golightly Harris, who assumed responsibility for their piedmont South Carolina farm and 10 slaves when David was called to military duty in November 1862. As he prepared to leave, David noted in his diary that Emily "has had but little experiance beyond her house-hold affairs" and prophesied accurately that she would "be much at a loss with the management of the farm and the negroes."[13]

On some places where the war brought a change in management it was not a white woman or man who took over but a black man. Burrel, who so ably oversaw matters on the Florida farm of Winston Stephens after Stephens joined the Confederate cavalry, was mentioned in chapter 1. Another slave entrusted with such responsibility was a young man named Andrew who lived on a Texas plantation owned by Bob Goodman. Andrew customarily did house duty, and Goodman came to know him well. Sensing considerable ability in Andrew despite his youth (he was only 22), Goodman decided that he could be trusted to "look after things" in his master's absence. As he prepared to go off to war in 1861, Goodman summoned his 66 slaves and made the surprising announcement: "I'm turnin' the overseer off and leavin' Andrew in charge of the place. . . . Now, you all mind what Andrew says." Confident of a quick Confederate victory, Goodman told the hands he would be back soon; but as it turned out he was gone for four years, during which time Andrew's managerial skills kept the place going.[14]

Even in their master's absence, however, many slaves remained subject to his scrutiny and his commands, for slaveowners in military service often received reports on affairs at home and directed matters at long distance through return letters. Although he thoroughly trusted Burrel, Winston Stephens solicited regular updates on his activities and included detailed instructions for him in letters home. "I want Burrel to plant corn soon," Stephens wrote his wife in February 1863, "and I want him to prepare the land well and manure all the pine land . . . I want him to finish planting corn by the 10th March and the cotton also if possible."[15]

Some slaves had reason to be thankful that their absent master still wielded power at home. When one of those on the Johns plantation in Chambers County, Alabama, complained to a white woman on the place that the overseer was abusive and had even whipped children, she wrote about it to the master, who was away in the army. His reply was unequivocal: fire the overseer.[16] Other slaves had less reason to be pleased with their owner's long-range oversight. One was a man named Peter, owned by the Bird family of Granite Farm plantation in Hancock County, Georgia. In the summer of 1863 he somehow incurred the displeasure of the plantation mistress. She wrote her husband, an army officer in Virginia, giving no details of the matter but suggesting that she would like to be rid of Peter. Her husband replied: "I agree cheerfully to what you wish about that fellow. Sell him by all means, and as far off as possible." He reiterated this in a letter nine days later: "[S]ell Peter. . . . [T]here should be no such negro on a place *in such times.*"[17]

The selling of slaves went on unabated in most parts of the South until the Confederacy collapsed. An efficient system of moving labor to where it was most needed was essential to slavery's profitability. Such a system had evolved before the war and continued during it. By means of sale, slaves were moved around within communities, within states, and from one state to another. The trade often exiled black people to places far from their home and loved ones.[18]

The prices paid for slaves in the Confederacy rose dramatically during the war. How much of this was fueled by supply-and-demand factors and how much by the drastic devaluation of the Confederate dollar is debatable, but whites touted the high prices and brisk trade as proof of slavery's health and the public's confidence in its future.[19] "Just at the very time, when Lincoln declares that [slaves] are to be emancipated," crowed the editor of a Staunton, Virginia, newspaper in January 1863, "they command higher prices than ever before. Could anything demonstrate more satisfactorily the futility of his infamous proclamation? The people of the South never felt that the institution of slavery was ever safer than at the present time." As evidence, he cited a recent auction in the nearby village of Greenville, at which 13 black people were disposed of: "A man aged twenty-five years and defective, $1,500; . . . woman and child, $1,500; girl, aged fourteen years, $1,500; . . . boy, twelve years, $1,605"; and so on.[20] Even as the Confederacy's end approached, the market held strong. An auction sale of 19 slaves in Moore County, North Carolina, in late December 1864 brought prices so high that one newspaper editor called them "ridiculous." They included $4,000 for 11-year-old Columbus, $3,800 for 9-year-old Silvey Jane, and $200 for 1-year-old Henderson. Only 59-year-old Silvey, described as "infirm," failed to bring a good price: she sold for $5.[21]

Many Southern whites were so used to this buying and selling of human beings that they gave little thought to the havoc it wreaked on its victims. Property was property, after all, and of course it had to be exchanged now and then. A Mississippi lawyer's diary entry for November 13, 1862, suggests how routine the selling of black people seemed to some whites: among his activities that day, he noted in passing, was preparing "a deed conveying two negroes, and two mules, and a wagon to Mrs. Malinda M. Bigbee."[22] A Texas newspaper editor told his readers of an estate auction in 1863 in which the 138 slaves for sale brought a total of $208,000. "Mules and oxen," he added, "also seemed to be in great demand."[23] A Richmond newspaper that surveyed the regional market in slaves in the fall of 1862 casually mentioned that children who were sold were sold with their mothers—"usually."[24]

Slaves themselves were not so insouciant about this trafficking in human beings that cruelly uprooted so many black people and tore them from family and friends. One who experienced the tragedy of forced separation was a boy named Morris, who was about nine years old when the war began and lived on a 20-slave plantation in Indian territory a few miles from the western border of Arkansas. His master (a Cherokee Indian), doubting the security of slave property in a country at war, decided to get rid of most of his. "In de second year of de War he sold my mammy . . . and my two brothers and my little sister," Morris recalled in his old age. "Mammy went to a mean old man named Peper Goodman and he took her off down de [Arkansas] river." His siblings went to a different buyer. He himself was kept on the plantation. The master also sold off Morris's aunt but kept his uncle, her husband. Not long afterward, Morris learned that his mother had died from rough treatment at the hands of her new owner.[25]

Another common practice that helped lubricate the business of slavery so that it ran smoothly and profitably was slave hiring. Some masters rented out one or more of their slaves, often those with special skills, to other whites who needed work done. Such slaves might be hired by the day, the month, or the year. Hiring of this sort did not generally take the slave far from home (though there were exceptions), and some hired slaves actually enjoyed the opportunity to be away from their master, although occasionally the hirers were abusive. Like slave sales, slave hiring continued unabated in most parts of the Confederate South during the war. Anthony, a carpenter who lived in Clarke County, Mississippi, was one engaged in such work. His owner had plenty of other slaves to work his plantation, so he hired Anthony out around the neighborhood, collecting the considerable sum of $1.50 a day for his craftsmanship with hammer, saw, and plane. This arrangement lasted until February 1863, when military authorities abruptly took Anthony away to labor with shovel and axe on fortifications more than 85 miles from home.[26] (Slaves hired out for war-related work had a different sort of experience, discussed in chapter 3.)

The farms and plantations of the mid-19th-century South were not just workplaces, of course. They were also homes where black people and white people carried on all the business of living. A much-cherished part of that business was the cycle of holidays, rituals, and festivities that brought rural folk together in celebration, observance, and relaxation. These gatherings were, more often than not, biracial. The war did not by any means put an end to them, although in some cases it altered them.

The fourth of July was traditionally a day of celebration and rest for blacks and whites in the rural South. Some masters, including planter Isaac Erwin of Iberville Parish, Louisiana, continued this custom during the war. "I gave the Negroes a fine Hog some Coffee Flour & sugar and Holliday to day," Erwin noted in his diary on July 4, 1864; "they [are] hav[ing] a big dinner."[27] Others, however, acknowledging the Confederate South's secession from the United States, abandoned that custom or substituted a different day. On the Watkins plantation in Carroll County, Mississippi, for example, Thursday the fourth of July 1861 came and went like any other day, but on Saturday the sixth all hands got the day off and enjoyed a feast.[28] Next in the traditional cycle came the laying-by time, which on some places meant not just less work but also festivities of various sorts. Cushing Hassell, a small slaveholder in Martin County, North Carolina, noted in his diary one such event on Tuesday, August 4, 1863. A planter who lived nearby had his overseer prepare a big dinner for everyone on the plantation and invited some of his neighbors to join in. "Nearly all [my] family both white and black went," Hassell wrote, "& the affair passed off quietly & apparently very satisfactory to the negroes."[29] Next in turn came the rituals that celebrated the end of the harvest. David Golightly Harris and his hands were among those who followed this custom. On November 13, 1861, with the crops all gathered and the last of the corn ears shucked, "The boys put me upon their sholders," as Harris wrote, and "carried me in a victorous mener around the house."[30]

Christmas was the favorite holiday of blacks and whites alike. Most masters allowed their hands several days off, gave them presents, and permitted them to join with others in the neighborhood in festivities. These yuletide customs continued during the war, although white fears about black insurrection sometimes restricted the festivities, and economic hardship often limited the gift-giving. On the Wadley plantation in Ouachita Parish, Louisiana, the day after Christmas was set aside for the hands' big holiday celebration. "The negroes are busy barbecueing and cooking for their party tonight," the master's daughter wrote in her diary on December 26, 1862. That night she again took up her pen to describe the scene: "I hear now the sounds of fiddle, tambourine and 'bones' mingled with the shuffling and pounding of feet. . . . [T]hey are having a merry time." The war introduced new rituals, too, notably the days of fasting and prayer that President Davis declared periodically and that many masters required their slaves to observe. Friday, March 27, 1863, was one of those days; the slaves on the Wadley plantation were given the day off by way of compensation for going hungry.[31]

The rituals and observances associated with the intimate human experiences— birth, marriage, death—likewise continued in the rural South during the war years. These too were generally biracial, for blacks and whites customarily paid their respects at one another's baptisms, weddings, and funerals. Black weddings were mostly simple ceremonies, like that which united Jim and Mary of Live Creek, Georgia, in 1863. A black lay preacher led the two through the exchange of vows; then, bidding Jim take Mary's right hand, he pronounced them "man and wife, by the Commandments of God. We shall hope and trust through God that you may live right." The voices of those assembled then rose in song, and the ceremony concluded.[32] But some masters indulged their slaves—especially favored house servants—with elaborate ceremonies. A white woman described one such event on a Louisiana sugar plantation in January 1862. The veranda of the Big House was the setting, and the master's son performed the ceremony. "The groom had on a suit of black, white gloves & tall *beaver*. The bride dressed in white swiss, pink trimmings & white gloves. The brides-maid & groom's man dress[ed] to correspond." After the ceremony all the hands assembled in one of the plantation's large outbuildings for a dance.[33]

Such joyous occasions were, inevitably, succeeded by somber ones. In that era of abysmal medical ignorance, sickness and death were omnipresent, striking young and old alike, often with great suddenness. Fortunate were those who lived long and had sufficient warning of death's approach to allow family and friends to see them off properly to the other world. Among the fortunate was Dinah, a house servant on a plantation in Burke County, Georgia. As her health failed in 1863, her husband Sam attended her lovingly. When she fell into a coma in late July, blacks from all over the neighborhood gathered at her bedside and remained until the end, singing hymns in beautiful harmony. Once her body was prepared for burial, they gathered again for the graveside service.[34]

Slave funerals, like slave weddings, were mostly plain affairs. Allen Parker described in his memoir the funeral of his mother, who died in North Carolina in August 1861:

> She was buried in the same manner that most of the slaves were. A negro carpenter made a rough pine box, without lining, trimming, or paint. Her only shrowd was a white night-dress, yet the tender hands of her loved ones smoothed this out as carefully

as if it had been of the finest satin. A few of the nearest friends and neighbors gathered round the rough coffin to take a last look at the dear face, then the cover was nailed on, the coffin placed in a cart and carried to a little sandy knoll, and beneath the shade of a few stunted pines a shallow grave was dug, in which without ceremony the coffin was placed and the sandy earth heaped above it.[35]

Death visited the rural South with increasing frequency as the war took its awful toll on the combatants. For some slaves, the most memorable of all the war's events was the death of their master or one of his sons at the front. Young Sam Kendricks, son of a Crawford County, Georgia, planter, was hit severely in the neck during one of the Virginia battles. His letters from the hospital, which his mother read to some of the slaves, gave hope that he was recovering; but then came word that he had succumbed to the wound. "Dey brung [his body] home all de way from Virginny," recalled a former slave on the place, "an' buried him in de grave-yard on de other side of de garden wid his gray clothes on him an' de flag on de coffin. . . . [D]ey called all de niggers in an' 'lowed dem to look at Mars Sam. I seen him an' he sure looked like he peaceful in he coffin with his soldier clothes on."[36] For Minerva Bendy, a slave on a Texas plantation who was about eight years old when the war began, the battlefield death of her master's son brought the first inkling of the terrible reality of war. Three quarters of a century later she could still recall how stunned and perplexed she had been by that death, which seemed to her so senseless.[37]

The war left in its wake not only corpses but also living human wreckage, and Southern blacks beheld a good deal of that, too. At the Hendricks plantation in Columbia County, Georgia, which sat on a thoroughfare that many sick and wounded Confederate soldiers traveled along, the plantation mistress set up an infirmary in her house to help them and ordered some of her younger slaves to assist. One was Ellen, who was about 12 at the time. "I saw plenty wounded soldiers," she recalled years later. "They would come stragglin' in, all sick or shot, an' sometimes we had a room full of 'em. . . . That Confed'rate War was the terriblest, awfullest thing."[38] Charley Hurt, another Georgia plantation slave of about the same age, saw all three of his master's sons come home from the war disabled: one with fever, one with a bullet wound that would not heal, and one crippled by the wheel of an artillery piece that ran over his leg.[39] And, as in all wars, there were psychological traumas as devastating as the physical. Sally Banks Chambers, a child on a Texas plantation during the war, told an interviewer long afterward about her master's oldest son, who "went crazy" in the army. "It was shell-shock like. Dey brung him back from de war dat way and as fur as I ever knowed he ain' never git no better."[40]

In a wartime world that seemed sometimes to defy understanding, many slaves found comforting answers in religion. Faith also drew together a supportive community that made slavery more bearable. Most slaves on the smaller places, along with a good many on the plantations, attended a local church with their master and his family, and many formally joined the church. These biracial country churches, most of which were Methodist, Baptist, or Presbyterian, not only offered Sabbath preaching and Christian fellowship but also disciplined their members to keep them on the path of rectitude. The minutes of a Presbyterian church in Jefferson County, Mississippi, record the experience of "Perry [a] servant of R. M. Buies & a member of this church" who in October 1863 was called before the elders to answer a charge of spiritual laxity. After making "acknowledgements of past unfaithfulness [and] appearing deeply penitent . . . he was suitably admonished . . . & warned against backsliding in future."[41] The slave Jack, a wayward member of Academy Baptist Church in Tippah County, Mississippi, did not get off so lightly. Convicted by the elders in May 1862 of "unfaithfulness in the marriage relation, . . . he was excluded from the fellowship of the church."[42]

The country churches were controlled by white elders, and the preachers were of course white, and some sought to use their church for racial ends as well as the pure glorification of God. At many a Sunday meeting the preacher directed a special message to the gallery or back pews where the blacks sat. A South Carolina Methodist minister named Shuford did so on Sunday, April 2, 1865, concluding his sermon, as one person in attendance recorded, with a forceful warning to the blacks against "lying, stealing, cursing, quarreling, etc., and alluding to the Yankees as 'sent by the devil.'"[43] Ministers also frequently reminded the black brethren that the Bible commanded servants to be faithful and obedient to their masters. Black churchgoers, however, generally drew their own lessons from the weekly Bible text and sermon, silently but firmly dismissing ministerial pronouncements that rang false.

It was common to hold Sunday services for plantation slaves on the plantation itself. Sometimes a white minister, having presided that morning at his church, would make an afternoon appearance at a plantation service in the neighborhood. In the absence of a white minister, a black lay minister (known as an exhorter) often preached; these sermons the slaves found much more satisfactory.[44]

In many Southern states the law required that at least one white person be in attendance at these meetings to ensure that nothing seditious was afoot, but such laws were not always obeyed.[45] If no whites were present the slaves felt more comfortable, but even under white observation they often gave free rein to themselves physically and emotionally. On one plantation in southwest Georgia there stood, in the slave quarters, a "Praise House" where Sunday services for the blacks were held, usually led by the exhorters Old Bob and Jim. A white woman who visited the plantation in the winter of 1864–65 attended some of the Praise House services and described them in her diary. She was struck especially by the folk hymns that the slaves sang, "little speritual songs," as they called them, which were published in no hymnal but instead came from the heart. One went thus:

> I meet my soul at de bar of God,
> I heerd a mighty lumber.
> Hit was my sin fell down to hell
> Jes' like a clap er thunder.

"The women," she wrote, "when they get excited with the singing, shut their eyes and rock themselves back and forth, clapping their hands."[46]

Periodically—most often during the laying-by time in late summer or soon after the harvest, before the weather turned cold—country preachers led revivals. These events, which were sometimes held outdoors and generally went on for days or even weeks with preaching day and night, were often ecumenical and almost always biracial. In the highly emotional atmosphere invariably stirred up at these revivals, many of those who had been seeking but had not yet found were seized by the holy spirit and converted on the spot.[47]

George Browder, a white Methodist preacher in a rural Kentucky community, told in his diary of one such revival, which began in the last week of July 1863 and was led not only by white preachers of the Methodist, Baptist, and Presbyterian faiths but also by an exhorter named Black George. Larger and larger crowds turned out as the revival gained momentum, Browder recorded, and the gatherings generated a frenzied emotional intensity. At times two meetings were going on simultaneously, a white preacher leading the whites to salvation while, nearby, Black George led the slaves. On August 2, Browder baptized a slave woman and a white woman in a pond and then "preached to the largest congregation I have preached to for years." On the fourth he wrote, "Our revival deepens & widens—older and harder sinners are crying for mercy. . . . I never saw all denominations work together so well before." By August 16, when the excitement finally began to subside, some 50 blacks and 100 whites had experienced conversion and begun their new lives in Christ.[48]

Faith also helped blacks endure the material privations that afflicted them increasingly as the war went on. The Confederate South—its foreign imports drastically reduced by the Union naval blockade, its internal system of distribution crippled by inadequate and deteriorating railroads and the interdiction of coastal shipping, its resources of corn and wheat and livestock diminished by the Union army invasion of Tennessee and Virginia, and its westernmost regions severed from the rest by Union control of the Mississippi River—was ravaged by shortages of food and other necessities. Rural folk suffered less than townsfolk on the whole, but no one was exempt from hardship.[49]

Before the war, Southern rural communities had been in large part self-sufficient, raising plenty of corn, wheat, hogs, cattle, cotton, and wool to meet their own needs (and often a considerable surplus for outside sale). However, as white men went off to the army, slave men went off to work on fortifications, and slaves of both sexes ran off to the Yankees, labor shortages curtailed agricultural production. In addition, the Confederate government seized a great deal of meat and grain and hides through taxation and impressment; most went to the army, as intended, but some simply went to waste because the collapsing transportation system failed to move it to the front efficiently, thus obliging the government to requisition even more from the producers. There were, moreover, certain essentials that the South had never produced in sufficient quantity and therefore had to import; among these were salt (necessary to preserve meat) and precision-manufactured items such as needles, pins, and cotton cards. Furthermore, some farmers and planters had by 1861 given up home textile production, junked their spinning wheels and looms, and come to rely on store-bought fabric (often imported from the North) to clothe themselves and their slaves.[50]

Shortages afflicted the Confederacy's rural populace by late 1861. Each year thereafter brought increasing hardship. "I am sorry to learn by your letter that bacon is so awfully high," a Confederate officer in Virginia wrote to his wife in South Carolina in April 1862. "You must tell the negroes that it is perfectly impossible to give them but a very little meat while it is so high. . . . Tell them it is very painful for me to have to shorten their allowances in this way—but I am forced to do it. . . . [T]ell them I shall expect them to submit to it without a murmur."[51] In some cases the white family monopolized the available provisions and cut the slaves' rations. A Mississippi plantation mistress complained in September 1862 that "Times are very hard here. Everything is very high. Meat can't be bought. We have very little bacon, none to give the negroes."[52] A planter in the Georgia lowcountry likewise reported food shortages in 1862, adding that his slaves were unable to supplement their diet by fishing as they had before the war because fish hooks were now unobtainable, as was the yarn used for fishing nets, while the lead weights for the nets had all been recast into bullets.[53]

Blacks and whites in regions invaded by the Union army endured the worst food shortages, for federal troops seized provisions and livestock voraciously wherever they marched in enemy territory. Virginians and Tennesseans, their states invaded early and long occupied by huge Union forces, were particularly hard hit; some experienced actual famine.[54] "Great God when will this cruel war end," exclaimed a west Tennessee planter in December 1862. "[A] large army has been with us nearly seven months—the crops of the country & stock all gone."[55] Hammett Dell, a teenage slave on a middle Tennessee farm during the war, recalled long afterward how he and the others on the farm had suffered in the wake of visitations by Yankee foragers: "There couldn't be a chicken nor a goose nor a year of corn to be found bout our place. It was sich hard times."[56]

Clothing shortages likewise plagued the wartime South. "[T]he evils of war are felt in the scarcity & high prices," a South Carolina planter wrote in October 1862.

"Shoes, blankets & clothes cannot be obtained for our negroes."[57] David Golightly Harris's wife, Emily, managing their South Carolina farm in his absence, tried with little success to keep their 10 slaves decently shod: "The negroes are wearing wooden bottom shoes," she noted in early 1865. "They wear out so soon there is not much economy in using them."[58] In some cases blacks simply had to go without. A white woman on a small place in Georgia wrote in 1864 that she and her husband and children were reduced to wearing the sorriest sort of shoes, while "The [four] negroes are bare footed. Shoes are not to be thought of for them."[59] A letter to the editor of a Houston paper published around that time claimed that on the plantations in that region "the negroes are almost in a state of nakedness" and urged planters who did not produce cloth at home to start doing so.[60]

Some planters did just that. Henry Gibbs, a boy on a Mississippi plantation during the war, recalled in later years how the textile shortage was dealt with on his place. His master had customarily purchased all the cloth he required from a merchant in Mobile, but when the blockade cut off imports he pulled some of his female hands out of the fields, one of them Henry's mother, and put them to work carding, spinning, dyeing, and weaving. In their desperation to secure clothing, many masters and slaves resorted to extraordinary measures. With the winter of 1862–63 approaching and his clothes inadequate, a 12-year-old boy named Oliver made daily trips to the local railroad depot at his mistress's bidding. There he collected the cotton lint that had come loose from bales being shipped to market. After gathering sufficient fiber he went to work carding and spinning it, skills he had learned earlier. He also unraveled scraps of flannel and other wool fabric that his mistress gave him. She then paid to have the cotton and wool thread woven. This yielded a total of 14 yards of light and heavy cloth, which Oliver subsequently cut and sewed (using a sewing machine being another of his skills), ultimately providing himself with enough clothing to last a full year.[61]

As the war exacted its physical and emotional toll and transfigured the South in other ways, the customary relations between blacks and whites on many farms and plantations were threatened. Masters who took seriously the responsibility to provide for their slaves often agonized over their diminishing ability to do so and faithfully endeavored to do whatever they still could.[62] South Carolina planter Henry William Ravenel was appalled by reports that some slaveowners in areas invaded by the Union army were fleeing and leaving their slaves behind. Firm in his belief that slaves needed their master, he regarded abandoning them as a sinful dereliction of duty and resolved to stay with his no matter what. "We have always believed we were right in maintaining the relation of master & slave for the good of the country & also for the benefit of the negro," he wrote. "[The slaves] have grown up under us, they look to us for support, for guidance & protection. . . . In the sight of God, we have a sacred duty to stand by them as long as they are faithful to us. We know that if left to themselves, they cannot maintain their happy condition."[63] Mary Jones, a Georgia plantation mistress, continued during the war to act on her belief that slaveowners were responsible for their bondsmen's spiritual as well as material welfare. When her slave Joe returned home gravely ill after laboring on fortifications in the spring of 1862, she was concerned enough to visit him in the slave quarters in order to have "a conversation with him about the state of his soul." Reminding him that in earlier years he had regularly attended the Sunday school she conducted for her slaves, she asked him hopefully "where he was now looking for salvation." His reply was gratifying: "Only to the Lord Jesus Christ."[64]

Kentuckian George Browder, who besides preaching Methodism and leading revivals operated a 143-acre farm worked by at least 10 slaves, was the very embodiment of slaveholder paternalism, earnestly shepherding his black people according to his lights through all the disruptions of war. These disruptions included the Union army occupation of Kentucky, which encouraged many slaves, including some of Browder's, to defy their master. Browder tried to meet each challenge with understanding and forbearance, as he saw it, always sparing the whip if he could secure obedience in some other way. "My man Abram to day was in a very ill humor," he recorded in his diary on September 11, 1862, "—& talked very insolently to me, threatening to leave & never return. I talked very positively but very reasonably to him & he acknowledged his fault & promised reformation, so I excused him—believing that he had been misled by some outside influence." Three months later came another challenge: "My hired boy Henry was very insolent, insulting—& defiant this morning when I reproved him mildly." Seeing no recourse but punishment, Browder regretfully tied Henry's hands and prepared to whip him, "but he begged piteously, confessed his fault & promised never to do so again . . . so I untied him & forgave him—as I hope to be forgiven." A year and a half later, when misfortune struck some of his slaves in the form of a fire that burned down their cabin and destroyed all their clothes and furniture and other belongings, Browder was deeply affected. "[M]y poor negroes," he lamented. "I feel very sorry for them & will help them as far as I can." The very next day he traveled to the nearest town to buy necessities to replace those they had lost. Two days after that, several of Browder's female cousins who lived nearby came over to help his wife "make up some more clothing for our poor negroes. Thank God for good friends."[65]

There were other masters, however, who reacted quite differently to the trials of war, abandoning whatever paternalistic solicitude they may once have felt and replacing it with bitter anger and abuse. One black woman who eventually escaped to the Yankees recounted an experience of this sort. Up to a certain point, she said, she was content to stay with her master and mistress, for they had been kind. Things changed abruptly, however, when Union invasion threatened their state: "[T]hen, peared-like they would like to kill us."[66] Wes Brady, a teenager during the war on the plantation of John Jeems in Texas, remembered that "Old Master Jeems was getting the papers and dispatches from the war all the time. When he read them he just grunted and say, 'I don't believe it; the Niggers will never get free.' He cussed and 'bused the Niggers more ever time he read in the papers that the Niggers was going to be free."[67] Midge Burnett of Georgia recalled that her master had never hit a slave "a single lick" until the day when word came that a Yankee invasion was imminent. In the excitement of the moment a slave named Mose cried out, "Lawd bless de Yankees." This was, unfortunately, overheard by the master, who became enraged. "God damn [the] Yankees," he roared, as he delivered a blow to Mose's face that knocked him down.[68]

The departure of a master for the army and the subsequent assumption of control by a newly hired overseer spelled unwelcome changes for the slaves on many a plantation. Among them were those on Jack Haley's cotton plantation in Texas. When Haley went off to war he hired a man named Delbridge to oversee the place. "After dat," recalled former slave Andy Anderson, "de hell start to pop, 'cause de first thing Delbridge do is cut de rations. . . . He half starve us niggers and he want mo' work and he start de whippin's." Many decades later, Anderson still burned with resentment at this treatment. "I guess dat Delbridge go to hell when he died, but I don't see how de debbil could stand him."[69]

However the war might be altering the circumstances of life in the rural South, most slaves continued to obey their masters or overseers and do their work as they always had. Some did so with resignation, seeing no other choice; others did so as a practical matter because they felt they had a stake in maintaining their home; a few did so gladly because they felt real affection for and loyalty to their owner.

Allen Parker, a North Carolina slave, exemplified this last sentiment. He recalled in his memoir that "as I had always been well treated by all the Parker family I had no feelings for any of them except love and respect. The plantation had always been my home when I was not [hired out] . . . so, that I felt as if in a measure I was one of the family." Thus, until the late summer of 1862 when his situation changed, he willingly did whatever the Parkers required of him.[70] David and Emily Harris's slaves were impelled (at times) by the practical motive. One day in 1864, when David was away in military service, Emily returned from an overnight trip to Spartanburg to find that some of the blacks had taken it upon themselves to skin two of the Harris cows that had wandered onto a neighbor's property and died from gorging on sugar cane. Had those valuable hides been left to go to waste, the slaves knew, it would have meant that much less shoe leather for them as well as the Harrises, and thus they took the initiative in their mistress's absence.[71] Slaves on William Patrick's large plantation in Ouachita Parish, Louisiana, exemplified both these motives. Plagued by Union army raiders who seized much of the provisions on the place, the slaves willingly dug a large pit at Patrick's bidding, secreted in it the remaining food supplies, and kept the secret from the Yankees. As one of those slaves, Aaron Russel, later testified, the blacks did this not only to keep from going hungry but also because they were fond of Patrick, an unusually kind master, and "want[ed] to he'p him."[72]

A few masters were indebted to their slaves for extraordinary acts of devotion. Stories of the "faithful slave" would become a much exaggerated and romanticized staple of the postwar legend of the Lost Cause, but they were not without a grain of truth. Three of Mary Jones's house servants (Flora, Tom, and Charles) repaid her concern for their spiritual and material welfare by protecting her during a disturbing episode in 1863. The recently widowed Jones was upstairs in the Big House, as she later related in a letter to her son, when a "suspicious-looking character" came to the door asking for a handout. Tom and Flora immediately took position in the doorway and prevented the man from entering the place even when he insisted on coming inside "to see how it looked." They also alerted their mistress and warned her not to come downstairs. She told them to feed the man, as Christian charity required, so Charles brought him a plate of rice and pork and a bowl of clabber. But he kept the man out on the piazza and gave him only a spoon to eat with, too suspicious even to put a knife or fork in his hands. The blacks kept a close eye on the stranger as he ate, and as soon as he finished "Charles politely told him if he would now start he would put him on the right road." The man left, whereupon Jones expressed her gratitude to her servants for their "ingenuity . . . and the protection afforded by them."[73]

Blacks came to the rescue in a terrifying incident one night in October 1862, when a pile of clothing left too close to the fireplace ignited in the bedroom where George Browder was asleep with his wife, Lizzie, and their youngest child, Luther. Two slave men owned by a neighbor happened to be passing by the house at that moment. Seeing what was happening they "rushed in & dragged the burning clothes into the yard," as Browder later recounted in his diary. But by then the fire was spreading through the bedroom, inflicting burns on Lizzie and threatening George and baby Luther. In an instant, two of Browder's own slaves appeared and helped him extinguish the flames. "[O]ur faithful Ellen & George came in to our relief just in bare time to save us from a fearful conflagration & possibly us & our children from a horrid death." Meanwhile, the hired boy Henry hurried off to fetch the doctor to treat Lizzie's burns. The Reverend Browder ascribed this "timely deliverance" fundamentally to "God's good providence," but was profoundly grateful to the blacks for acting as His instruments.[74]

A great many slaves, however, felt no attachment to their master or mistress and no interest in the work they were forced to do. While open disobedience was prohibitively risky for most such blacks, some found safe ways to resist. One was Andy Anderson of Texas, who was sold off the Haley plantation after the hated overseer Delbridge took over only to find that his new owner, a planter named House, was no less abusive than

Delbridge. After a particularly savage beating by House's overseer, Anderson made up his mind not only to do as little work as he could get away with but also to commit sabotage whenever he could: "If I seed de cattle in de cornfield, I turns [my] back, 'stead of chasin' 'em out."[75] Theft was another covert way of striking back at a master or at whites in general, and there was a good deal of that during the war, too, much of it stimulated by the shortages that slaves endured. Emily Harris noted in late 1864 that "Several negroes belonging to our neighbors have been stealing on [a] small scale to the great annoyance of their owners and others. Times are getting more desperate everyday."[76] Slaves on a South Carolina plantation not only plundered the vegetable stores, which their mistress found "aggravating," but also engaged in another common subterfuge: faking illness to avoid work. "I have had 24 cases of make believe sickness to prescribe for," the mistress wrote disgustedly, "the fever invariably having 'just gone off' and recurring always at night."[77]

Malingering, theft, sabotage, and other quiet acts of resistance had been around as long as slavery, of course, but the war offered some disaffected slaves additional opportunities to defy their oppressors. On those places where a white woman not used to directing slaves or agricultural work was forced to take over in the master's absence, such opportunities were common. David and Emily Harris's slaves, for example, although they willingly did chores that benefited them directly, such as skinning the dead cows, took advantage of David's absence and Emily's inexperience to set their own pace and agenda with regard to other farm work.

David had worried, as he departed for military service in mid-November 1862, that Emily would be "much at a loss" to handle her new responsibilities. His fears were realized. Hog-killing and butchering and salting between late November 1862 and the first of January 1863 went smoothly, for the slaves had a vested interest in laying in a good supply of meat for the coming year, but soon thereafter Emily began complaining of problems. On January 6 she admitted in her diary that "[T]hings dont go on like they did when [David] was at home." Although David periodically returned on leave and straightened matters out, his repeated absences brought more trials for Emily. She got particularly vexed at Christmastime 1864, when the slaves, who as always had been granted a certain amount of time off for the holiday along with permission to visit friends and kinfolk in the neighborhood, began abusing the privilege. "I have been very much provoked by the negroes leaving home without leave and staying over their time," she wrote on December 30. She lacked the confident sense of mastery, however, not to mention the physical strength, to administer the sort of punishment that her husband would have dealt out. This she confessed a few days later, after a scuffle between two of the slaves that ended with 16-year-old York beating up 49-year-old Will. "York must be corrected for fighting the old negro," she wrote, but "there is no one willing to do it for me." By February 1865 she had mustered the determination to inflict corporal punishment, but her feeble efforts did little to keep the slaves disciplined. "I had a fight with old Will," she wrote on the 22nd, "and hurt myself worse than him. It is a painful necessity that I am reduced to the use of a stick but the negroes are becoming so imprudent [i.e., impudent] and disrespectful, that I cannot bear it."[78]

Work continued on the Harris farm, but never at the pace Emily demanded. In March 1865 she again complained about the blacks; they were, she said, "very troublesome."[79] Such scenes were enacted on thousands of farms and plantations across the South in the war years, as white women found themselves arguing and negotiating with increasingly unruly slaves and sometimes simply throwing up their hands in frustration.[80]

On some places, even where a forceful master or overseer was present, obedience and discipline nearly broke down altogether. These instances occurred most often in areas so close to the Union lines that legal and institutional controls were disrupted and slaves could flee to the invaders without great risk if they chose to. Such was the case in the coastal North Carolina county of Hyde, which was vulnerable to Union Navy visitations and lay not far from the army-occupied town of Plymouth. A semiliterate overseer in that county sent a report to his absent employer in late December 1862 that painted a picture of virtual anarchy: "[T]he negroes act as thoe thay ware free[.] [S]ome dayes weay cant get more than a haff douzin [of the men] to worcke. . . . [Most of] the negroes that ware hired out . . . are lyinge round the quarters ore in the swampe[.] [Y]ou now this is tryinge to me thoe I get a longe withe ite the beste I can."[81] Gloucester County, Virginia, in that state's tidewater region, was in a comparable situation and experienced a similar derangement of the labor system. "My negroes behave pretty well," Gloucester planter Colin Clarke remarked sarcastically in September 1862. "They get up when they please, & work as they please. . . . I direct what I wish done, & they do it at their perfect leisure & convenience." Discipline on the place continued to deteriorate, as Clarke reported a year later. Fearing that if he tried to force the blacks to work harder they would simply pack up and go to the Yankees, he let them "do pretty much what they please," which was "little or nothing." He was afraid to rebuke them even when they displayed outright "insolence": "I pretend not to notice it."[82]

Thoroughgoing disorder of this sort was the exception rather than the rule, however, as was even the lesser disruption on the Harris place. On the great majority of Southern farms and plantations, at least in the Confederate states, slaves found no way to loosen the bonds of slavery or strike back at their masters beyond the covert tactics they had always employed. In other words, the war brought no fundamental change in their relations with whites. The power of the master or overseer, backed by the will of the white community and the formal and informal institutions of racial control, remained in most parts of the rural South unchallengeable, and slaves remained slaves until the Confederacy was no more.

The whip continued to be the primary instrument with which whites compelled obedience, deterred resistance, and punished insubordination. The slaves on David Harris's farm were as familiar with it as most others were. One day in early March 1862, for example, Harris gave young York "a genteel floging," as he described it in his diary, "for leaving home without orders. He is becoming a little wild and needs close watching."[83] There was nothing "genteel" about the punitive floggings that many other slaves received. Andy Anderson retained all his life a vivid memory of the brutal punishment that set him on a path of quiet resistance on the House plantation in Texas. Anderson's offense in this instance was accidentally running over a tree stump and thereby damaging the wagon in which he was hauling firewood. The overseer was "powe'ful mad" about this, Anderson remembered; his response was to tie Anderson to the plantation whipping post and give him 10 hard lashes on his bare back. That was only the beginning, however. He left Anderson tied to the post for 4 hours, returning every 30 minutes to deliver another 10 lashes. The pain was excruciating for the first couple of hours, Anderson recalled, but after that he passed into a state of semiconsciousness and his body went numb. The last thing he remembered clearly about the ordeal was "wishin' fo' death." He was bedridden for two days after this torture and bore the scars all his life.[84]

When whipping failed to achieve the desired result, many slaveowners resorted to the auction block. Cushing Hassell of eastern North Carolina, for example, who by the standards of the time was a humane master, sold a refractory slave in February 1865. Her name was Harriet, and according to Hassell, "She was a great strumpet, lazy & impudent & whipping did not reform her in the least." He sent her to Greensboro to be auctioned off by a slave dealer. But his conscience would not let him separate her from her child; the little one went to Greensboro with her.[85] Many other masters were not so considerate.

The instruments of slave control served their purpose well in most parts of the Confederate South until after the last Rebel military forces laid down their arms. As late as the second week of May 1865—a month after Robert E. Lee's army surrendered in Virginia and two weeks after Joseph Johnston's army surrendered in North Carolina—Cushing Hassell's black people were laboring dutifully in his fields, slaves still; the eighth day of that month found them alongside their master and his sons planting potato sprouts.[86] In sections of the Confederacy more remote from Union occupation forces, May 1865 came and went with no change in the status of blacks. Such was the case in the piedmont South Carolina community where the Harrises lived. David returned from military service in the early spring of that year and quickly restored the discipline that Emily had let slip away. Plowing, planting, and hoeing then proceeded as they always had under his direction, and the slaves gave no trouble. On June 5, David heard that the Union general whose command included South

Carolina had issued a proclamation ordering the citizens to recognize the end of slavery: "I do not much think it will have much effect," he commented.[87]

Slavery did not survive much longer on the Harris place or any other place, contrary to David's prediction. Blacks everywhere in the rural South were soon celebrating their freedom. Celebrating, too, were blacks whose wartime experience had not been confined to farm or plantation. Their story is the subject of chapter 3.

THREE

❦

BEYOND THE
PLANTATION

Only a small minority of Southern slaves lived and worked outside the realm of agriculture before the Civil War, and such slaves remained a minority during the conflict. But their numbers grew after the spring of 1861, as the Confederacy created a war machine and drew on the enslaved population for nonagricultural service of various kinds, much of it in towns and cities. Moreover, a large minority of the South's free blacks lived in urban areas before and during the war. Slaves who moved from agricultural work to war work experienced substantial changes in their lives, as did urban blacks as the war went on. In addition, between 1861 and 1865 many thousands of slaves were uprooted by their owners as an emergency measure, taken abruptly from the plantation, farm, village, town, or city that was their home to a faraway place safe from Yankee invaders.

Among the blacks who experienced the war most intensely were those who accompanied their owner or one of his sons to the Confederate army as body servants. Thousands of enslaved boys and young men served in this capacity. Most had been house servants before the war, typically on a big plantation (big enough, that is, to spare a slave for army duty). These military body servants, or "bodyguards" as they called themselves, were not provided for by the army but were instead personally subsisted by the white soldiers they served, who were generally officers and men of substantial means.[1]

Body servants' duties were many. Because officers were required to provide their own rations, those with servants often assigned them to procure food. A South Carolina boy named Abram, whose owner, Major James Griffin, took him along to the army in Virginia, proved to be a resourceful forager. Griffin would give him money and a signed pass and then send him off to buy provisions from local farms; Abram would return laden with sweet potatoes, butter, poultry, and the like. "He is a first rate Boy," Griffin wrote his wife in April 1862, "I think more of him than I ever did."[2] Body servants also chopped firewood, cooked meals, did laundry, polished shoes and uniform buttons, gave haircuts and shaves, cleaned and repaired arms and equipment, cared for horses, helped construct winter-quarters cabins, and performed other personal chores for the officers they served.[3]

Body servants also shared in the hardships and dangers of army life. John McAdams, who was about 12 and living on a middle Tennessee plantation when the war began, told an interviewer long afterward about his years as a body servant in the army. He remembered campaigning in blisteringly hot weather and enduring "terrible times when we didn't have a thing to eat but green corn for 2 weeks at a time and we would not have water to drink for 3 or 4 days either." On occasion he drank muddy water that had collected in a low spot in the ground, as grateful for it as if "it was the best water in the world." Like most other body servants, McAdams was kept well to the rear during battles, but even there he found the noise so deafening that he had to stuff cotton in his ears to bear it.[4] A few got closer to the battle lines. William Coleman of west Tennessee, a mere boy of fewer than 12 years, was required, along with other body servants, to carry wounded men back from the front lines during lulls in the fighting. "[W]hile part of us seen after the wounded," he recalled, others "would have to go and dig out a long ditch, roll the dead ones in and cover them over."[5] Some body servants made the ultimate sacrifice. One was Levy Moore, who left his home plantation in Texas to accompany two of his master's sons to war. "He was struck wid de fever at Sabine Pass," as a niece of his remembered, "and die[d] right dere."[6]

Sharing privation and peril in the insular, all-male world of the army forged powerful bonds between some body servants and the soldiers they served. Many such slaves persevered devotedly through the war, ignoring opportunities to escape. Henry Smith of Texas was one. He went to war in 1861 with Jim Smith, his owner's son, who served in the famed Texas Brigade of Lee's army. Although in his later years Henry referred to the conflict as the "Freedom War," it brought him no freedom until well after the surrender of the Confederate armies. He served "Marse Jim" faithfully through the Texas Brigade's many campaigns—until October 1864, when Jim fell in battle near Richmond. After burying Jim's body, Henry made the long trek back to Texas on a mule, carrying the news of Jim's death and a few of his possessions to Jim's family. War's end found Henry at work on his home plantation.[7] Other blacks, however, proved less dedicated to body-servant duty. Not long after Abram was praised as a "first rate Boy" by Major

Griffin in Virginia, he began losing interest in foraging and repeatedly disappointed the major, who therefore found it necessary "to scold him on two or three occasions" and finally to administer "a light flogging."[8]

Many thousands of slaves served the Confederate army in capacities other than body servant. In cities such as Charleston where sizeable military forces were permanently stationed to man defensive works, local slaves were often informally hired by soldiers as camp cooks or laundresses. Many more slaves were hired formally from their masters by various War Department agencies, including the Quartermaster and Commissary bureaus, which had depots, warehouses, wagon-repair shops, bakeries, slaughterhouses, meat-packing plants, and facilities of other sorts at hundreds of locations throughout the Confederate states. Some of these blacks worked as common laborers or wagon drivers while others held skilled jobs. In Lynchburg, Virginia, where the Quartermaster bureau oversaw a complex of shops and warehouses, nearly 300 hired slaves were employed. Among them were teamsters, laborers, ropemakers, shoemakers, wheelwrights, carpenters, blacksmiths, boat makers, boatmen, tanners, and cooks. At other Quartermaster facilities slave artisans made harnesses for draft animals and shoes for soldiers.[9]

Some of the slaves hired for Quartermaster or Commissary duty, particularly teamsters, were assigned to Confederate forces in the field. Between body servants and hired slaves, a major field force such as the Army of Northern Virginia in the eastern theater or the Army of Tennessee in the western had at any given time thousands of black men marching or driving in its ranks and camping in its bivouacs. This fact has doubtless contributed to the myth, devoutly upheld in certain circles today, of the "black soldiers of the Confederacy," that is, the notion that large numbers of blacks served voluntarily in the Rebel ranks as combat soldiers. There is no substance to this myth. It happened occasionally that a body servant picked up a musket in the heat of battle and fought side by side with the Rebel soldiers, and there is scattered evidence suggesting that a few slaves and free blacks served willingly as soldiers in combat units, some as sharpshooters. Moreover, at the war's outbreak some free-black men in several cities, including Richmond, Mobile, and New Orleans, offered their services to the Confederacy as soldiers. Fourteen hundred in New Orleans actually organized themselves into companies of "Native Guards," armed and uniformed mainly at their own expense, and were formally incorporated into the Louisiana militia. One or more free-black companies apparently formed in Mobile as well. However, the Confederate government refused to accept free-black units in the army and none ever left its city of origin or saw combat as Rebel troops. (After the federal capture of New Orleans in 1862 the Native Guards volunteered for, and were mustered into, the Union army, and thereafter saw action in various locations.) In the war's last weeks, after the Confederate Congress reluctantly approved enlisting slaves as combat troops, as many as a couple of hundred—but more likely just a few dozen—were recruited and began training in Richmond; the Confederacy's collapse intervened, however, before they saw any action.[10]

Although blacks did not bear arms for the Confederacy in meaningful numbers, there is no denying that black muscle and skill, however unwillingly provided, significantly strengthened the Confederate war effort. War Department agencies other than the Commissary and Quartermaster bureaus also hired slaves, as did agencies of the Navy Department. Moreover, hundreds of private firms and institutions, along with all 11 Confederate states, put slaves to work at jobs essential to maintaining the Rebel armies. As the war went on and the Confederacy was forced to put more and more white men into the military ranks, slave labor played an increasingly important role in supporting the armies.[11]

Thousands of slaves helped to produce arms and ammunition. Some worked for private industrial establishments such as the small Griswold Pistol Factory in Georgia, which hired a few dozen, or the huge Tredegar Iron Works in Richmond, which hired hundreds to help manufacture cannons and shells. Other slaves made muskets and cartridges in the numerous armories and arsenals operated by the War Department's Ordnance bureau. The raw materials for these munitions were likewise produced by both private and government facilities that employed slaves extensively, including the numerous iron furnaces owned by entrepreneurs in Virginia's Shenandoah Valley and the lead mines and saltpeter caves throughout the South exploited by the War Department's Niter and Mining bureau.[12]

Some of the work done at these sites was familiar to blacks who came from plantations—teamstering, for instance—but much was unfamiliar. Moreover, certain jobs could be done by women as well as men, and women were therefore hired in considerable numbers at some facilities. Among the nearly 200 slaves employed at the Ordnance bureau's Arkadelphia Arsenal in Arkansas in early 1863 were 41 men and women hired from Thomas Swift, who was likely a planter, perhaps one forced to flee from an invaded region and find other employment for his hands. The Swift slaves at the arsenal included Milton, Brim, and Saunders, who made bullets; Mary, Flora, Henry, and Ike, who assembled cartridges; Billy, Jim, and Tom, common laborers; Moses, a wagoner; and Eliza and Maria, cooks.[13]

Some slaves hired at munitions-related works were skilled men who had learned their trade in the prewar years—carpenters, blacksmiths, wheelwrights, iron puddlers, charcoal makers, machinists, and so forth. Such men were in great demand and commanded a high price. One was Ed Taylor, a blacksmith at the Tredegar Iron Works, whose task was to hammer out the heavy iron bands used to reinforce the breeches of cannons. His master received $1,000 for his services at Tredegar in 1863, five times the annual hiring price of a common laborer.[14]

At Tredegar and many other ordnance works, supervisors preferred the carrot to the stick as a means of encouraging the productivity of slave labor. At these facilities, while the threat of the whip was always there, its sting was rarely felt except as punishment for theft, drinking, card playing, direct disobedience of orders, or other such rule violations. Instead, positive incentives—generally in the form of cash bonuses paid directly to the slaves, which they were free to spend as they wished—encouraged workers to do their tasks willingly and energetically. Ed Taylor, for instance, was enticed by cash incentives to work more than his contract required. For each day he worked beyond the required 24 per month he received $7.50 along with $6.00 for each breech band he wrought; in January 1864 alone, he earned the considerable sum of $127.50. Most of the other slaves at Tredegar took advantage of similar, if less lucrative, offers. So too at other ordnance works, including the Confederate armory in Macon, Georgia, where even the common laborers could earn a good bit of spending money; those who dug clay for brick-making, for example, were required to dig 20 cubic yards per day but were allowed to dig up to 5 more at 20 cents per yard if they did it before the end of the 10-hour workday. Among the things that slaves might purchase with their earnings were tobacco, food delicacies, and fancy items of clothing.[15]

Another crucial manufacturing enterprise in which slaves participated extensively was salt-making. Salt is important for the health of humans and animals and was essential in preserving meat in the prerefrigeration era. Before the Civil War, Southerners had generally relied on foreign sources of salt, but the Union naval blockade forced them to turn to their own. The Confederate government took no part in this endeavor, instead leaving the matter up to individuals and the states. Many masters dispatched slaves to the Gulf or south Atlantic coasts, where they boiled down seawater in large kettles. The underground salt deposits at Saltville, Virginia, were another source that slaves helped exploit, as was the saline groundwater found in Clarke County, Alabama. The Alabama state government set up a large salt-making operation in Clarke County that employed hired slaves of both sexes, some 200 or more. The men bored the wells that tapped the subterranean brine, tended the steam-powered pumps that brought it to the surface, manned the furnaces where the brine was boiled down, chopped the wood that fueled the furnaces, and dried and sacked the salt; the women cooked, did laundry, and tended the seven-acre garden that provided fresh vegetables for the hands.[16]

Moving salt, munitions, foodstuffs, and other essential goods from the producers to the soldiers and civilians who needed them made enormous demands on the Confederacy's transportation system. Here, too, hired slaves were put to work in great numbers, serving on river boats, canals, and especially railroads. Slaves had done such work before the war, but the growing scarcity of white civilian men in the war years thrust slaves into a more prominent role. Both the skilled and the unskilled were employed (but men only, in this case). The Virginia Central Railroad, for example, hired in 1861 some 168 slaves for its track-repair gang and another 100 for other jobs, including unskilled woodchoppers and highly skilled brakemen, firemen, mechanics, and boilermakers; a year later 223 slaves were at work on the track-repair gang alone.[17]

Hired slaves also contributed to the Confederate war effort by working in military hospitals. The War Department's Medical bureau established some 200 general hospitals at locations throughout the Confederate states; sick and wounded soldiers were also treated in hospitals set up by state authorities and private charitable associations. Both female and male slaves worked in these hospitals, serving in various capacities but mostly as unskilled help. In the army general hospitals, many slave men and some slave women tended the patients directly as nurses (considered an unskilled job in those days). Under the direction of white ward matrons, the nurses (1 was assigned to every 10 beds) distributed rations and medicine to the patients, bathed them, changed their clothing and bed linen, cleaned bedpans and privies, mopped and dusted the wards, aired mattresses, and carried nonambulatory patients from train depot to ward. Other enslaved men chopped firewood, tended livestock, and buried the dead, while other enslaved women cooked, did laundry, made soap, and tended gardens.[18]

Hospital work was not for the squeamish. It took a stout heart to endure the sights, sounds, and smells of the wards, where soldiers lay suffering from ghastly diseases and from wounds in every conceivable part of their bodies. One young slave woman who visited a military hospital in Atlanta on a number of occasions in the company of her mistress still vividly recalled, many decades later, the horror of it. "[D]e men was always screaming an' groaning an' taking on an' it stuck in my ears," she told an interviewer. "I could hear 'em all night [after] I wen[t] dere in de day time."[19]

Many slaves put to work for the Confederate war effort—probably the majority—were not willingly hired out by their masters but instead were impressed by state or Confederate authorities. All but a few of these impressed slaves were men, and nearly all were assigned to unskilled labor duty. A small proportion did railroad work and the like (the Confederate government provided more than a hundred to the Virginia Central Railroad in 1864, for example, to reinforce the track-repair gang), but the vast majority were used to construct the extensive earthwork fortifications that protected many Confederate cities and other key points.[20]

In the war's first months some masters volunteered slaves for such labor duty. Indeed, South Carolina masters sent slaves to work on fortifications around Charleston as early as December 1860, immediately after the state's secession. As time went on, however, the authorities' demand for such laborers grew and masters became less enthusiastic about providing them, particularly during the busy months of planting, cultivating, and harvesting. The War Department's Engineer bureau hired some slaves by the year to work on fortifications, but could never secure enough of them in that manner. Eventually the Confederate Congress and states authorized the impressment of slaves for limited periods (typically 30 or 60 days) and with compensation to the owner.[21]

Such forcible appropriation of black labor angered slaveowners. Many protested, some dragged their feet in complying, a few resisted outright. "I suppose I will be compelled to send one [or more] of our negroes," Emily Harris wrote in April 1864, after receiving word that the authorities were demanding thousands of able-bodied male hands to work on South Carolina's coastal fortifications, "but they shall not budge till they are literally compelled to go."[22] Alfred Quine, overseer of a plantation near Vicksburg, Mississippi, hid all his employers' slaves in the woods when an army impressment squad came around in February 1863. Nevertheless, the number of slaves who labored on Rebel fortifications at one time or another was very large, certainly many tens of thousands, perhaps hundreds of thousands. In November 1862, for example, 4,150 were sent from 26 Virginia counties to construct fortifications around Richmond, only 400 fewer than the Confederate government had called for. In the early weeks of 1863 2,000 impressed slaves were at work on the fortifications protecting Savannah, and at least 10,000 Alabama slaves were impressed prior to August 1863 to build defensive works at Mobile and other points in south Alabama.[23]

Laboring on earthworks displeased the laborers themselves as least as much as their masters. It was very hard work with pick and shovel and axe under highly regimented conditions, often in unhealthy locations such as mud flats or swamps. The stick, rather than the carrot, was the rule in these army labor gangs, and some of the soldiers assigned to supervise them employed the whip or strap even more readily than the overseers and masters back home.[24] A Georgia man named Tines Kendricks remembered his days as an impressed laborer this way: "[I]t was something awful. De strap, it was goin' from 'fore day till 'way after night. . . . [H]eaps of [laborers] just fall in dey tracks give out an' them white men layin' de strap on dey backs without ceastin'."[25] Impressed slaves were supposed to get the same food allotment as Confederate soldiers, but this was in many cases less than they were used to at home and the army sometimes failed to provide the full ration. In addition, some of the food was barely edible. An army surgeon who investigated the condition of blacks laboring on the Mobile fortifications in 1863 found that the fresh beef and vegetables the men were supposed to get regularly were scarce, and thus "for as many as five and six days in succession the negroes have lived upon Bread and Molasses. The Corn Meal is issued in sufficient quantities, but there being no lard or fat of any kind issued it makes very unpalatable bread."[26] Moreover, some impressed laborers were taken from their homes so abruptly that their masters could not clothe them properly, and they consequently suffered from exposure, sometimes aggravated by inadequate shelter in leaky tents or drafty shanties and poor medical attention. Other laborers were held beyond their designated time. Not a few deserted and made their way back home, where they complained to their masters of abuse.[27]

Not surprisingly, the Confederate army's labor gangs were decimated by illness. Pneumonia and other diseases struck down workers by the thousands, many fatally. One who succumbed was the 35-year-old Clarke County, Mississippi, carpenter named Anthony (mentioned in chapter 2) whose master, planter Reese Price, customarily hired him out around the neighborhood. In March 1863 Price complied reluctantly but dutifully with the authorities' latest call by equipping Anthony with axe, shovel, blanket, cooking utensils, and three days' rations and turning him over to the local impressment agent, who took him off to work on the fortifications at Columbus. Anthony was quite healthy at that point, according to his master, but at Columbus he suffered from "exposure" and "sickened and died."[28]

Slaves laboring on fortifications around besieged cities faced lethal danger not only from disease but also from Yankee artillery fire. Jacob Stroyer, a young South Carolinian, very nearly lost his life this way. Taken from his piedmont plantation home to Charleston, he was put to work with other impressed slaves shoring up the defenses of Fort Sumter, which sat on a tiny man-made island in the city's harbor and became a Confederate bastion after its surrender in April 1861. Because the fort was regularly shelled by Union forces during the day, Stroyer and his fellow laborers worked at night, transported from the city out to the fort by boat after sunset and transported back before daybreak. One evening in July 1864, shortly after Stroyer arrived at the fort with a dozen or so others, a watchman on the wall spotted the sparking fuse of an artillery shell as it arced through the dark sky. When he shouted "look out," the slaves scurried to a nearby hut for shelter. But the shell came down directly on the hut and exploded. A fragment sliced into Stroyer's face, wounding him badly. He survived; all but one of the others died.[29]

Slaveowners heatedly protested the mistreatment of impressed laborers, angered not only by their own pecuniary sacrifice but also by the suffering of the bondsmen. In a letter dated December 17, 1864, a Virginia farmer voiced his complaint directly to the Confederate Secretary of War. Slaves in his county who had been impressed in early October to work on the Richmond fortifications for 30 days, he reported, had not yet been returned. Now the weather was turning cold, and the laborers' masters had not furnished them with warm clothes. Furthermore, he said, "We know from past experience and observation that negros impressed for the fortifications are generally badly treated and suffer much. . . . It is then no longer a question of property and value but of justice and humanity."[30]

Impressed laborers were not the only slaves who faced hazards and hardships when they left home to take up war work. The travails of the body servants at the front have already been noted. Slaves hired by the Confederate government, the states, or private firms also took risks. Peter and Alexander, the property of a South Carolina woman who hired them to the Wilmington & Manchester Railroad in North Carolina, were among the many victims of wartime railroad accidents. On a dark night in February 1862 they and three white men were manning a handcar, returning to the Wilmington depot after spending the day repairing the Brunswick River trestle. As they rounded a bend, a locomotive with six cars unexpectedly came at them from the opposite direction. The train was traveling in reverse, in preparation for moving onto a turnout just beyond the bend, and thus its headlight gave no warning. The handcar was crushed and those on it horribly mangled. The white men were killed instantly and Peter died later; Alexander sustained an ankle injury, but survived. A hired slave named Randall lost his life in a horrendous explosion in Richmond on the morning of November 23, 1864. It happened at a storage site where the army stockpiled large artillery shells. Randall was one of a number of black men dispatched to the site to load 30-pound shells into wagons for shipment to the front lines. Suddenly, and for no apparent reason, several of the shells exploded, hurtling red-hot fragments in all directions, fatally shattering the bodies of Randall and two other laborers, and badly injuring another, along with their white superintendent.[31]

War work inflicted emotional as well as physical wounds. Many families were separated for extended periods when slaves were sent off to labor in a distant place; separated, too, were the close-knit communities of the plantation slave quarters. A white woman described the poignant scene on her Mississippi plantation in early December 1862, when a number of slaves were sent away to work for a whole year on an Alabama railroad: "I have never witnessed as much distress and so many tears as was shown and shed the morning they left. There was not a dry eye on the place, even the negro men cried like children." When Christmas came a few weeks later, there was none of the customary merriment in the slave quarters of that plantation.[32] Homesickness and depression were common among slaves taken away for long periods. Fortunate indeed were the ones hired out as families or whole communities, such as those Thomas Swift sent to the Arkadelphia arsenal.[33]

Many slaves hired out for war work found themselves for the first time living in an urban environment. The towns and cities of the South had been home to only a small minority of slaves before the war (about 1 of 20, based on the Census Bureau's 1860 definition, which awarded urban status to places with more than 2,500 inhabitants), but that proportion grew substantially during the war as rural slaves were sent by their masters to take jobs in urban factories, workshops, depots, and hospitals, and others were brought in by masters fleeing the invaded regions. Many slaves who came to towns and cities from the countryside also found themselves for the first time in the presence of large numbers of free blacks.[34]

The privations that afflicted rural folk in the Confederate South took an even greater toll on urban folk, black and white. Few town or city people had even so much as a small vegetable garden to supplement their food supply, and thus most were entirely dependent on purchases. The wartime urban population boom multiplied the pressure on the dwindling food resources. "During de War things was so high dat you couldn't 'ford to buy nothing," recalled the former slave Ella Belle Ramsey, who had lived in Atlanta in those years. "I 'member one time Mis' Goldsmith [her mistress] fuss 'cause dey try to charge her five dollars for a little dab of sugar. I hear her say dat somebody tol' her dat dey sell potatoes an' carrots for a dollar each one."[35] Urban population growth also spawned severe housing shortages and high rents. "The very negroes in the streets are talking of the hard times," a white woman in Charleston observed in the spring of 1862. Another Charlestonian overheard a black man in the city exclaim that same spring,

"'Hard times—yes, they is so hard, that I think they are almost as bad as the day of judgment.'"[36] Urban crowding fostered disease, too, especially in the sickly season from late summer through fall. Epidemics swept many towns and cities during the war. Yellow fever, for example, hit Wilmington, North Carolina, in September 1862, killing 650 people over the next two months, 150 of whom were black.[37]

Life was not, however, altogether grim for the black residents of the Confederacy's towns and cities. For one thing, urban slaves enjoyed certain liberties that their rural brethren did not—customs that long predated the war and continued during it. Although the practice violated municipal codes, many slaves in towns and cities "hired their own time," that is, with their owner's consent they sold their services to other whites, made the contractual arrangements on their own, and lived on their own (sometimes in all-black neighborhoods), merely meeting with their owner now and then to turn over an agreed-upon portion of their earnings. In the town of Canton, Mississippi, for example, three slave men belonging to the widow Sarah Garrett hired their own time in the early part of the war, one of them as a barber and the others as draymen. Many of the slaves hired informally as camp cooks and laundresses by troops stationed in Charleston and other cities were hiring their own time. Such slaves were living for all intents and purposes as free blacks, but the practice suited their masters because it relieved them of the responsibilities of slave management and care while still profiting them financially.[38]

Self-hire, along with the overtime system that prevailed in the munitions factories and certain other places where slaves were employed, put a good deal of cash into the pockets of enslaved men and women in towns and cities. Other urban slaves earned spending money by peddling pies and other treats to hungry soldiers who were stationed in or near the towns or who passed through on the railroads.[39]

A few slaves took advantage of wartime conditions to line their pockets through theft. Richmond, with its vast concentration of Confederate government and military facilities, offered especially rich pickings. William and Lewis, slaves employed at the Winder General Hospital in the city, stole clothing from the hospital's supply room over a period of time in 1863—apparently intending to sell it rather than wear it, for they reportedly took enough to fill a large wagon. Black Quartermaster and Commissary teamsters hauling forage and provisions and other goods around the city pilfered so much from their cargoes that the authorities were forced by early 1864 to institute a system of weighing each wagon upon loading and unloading. Other black Richmonders served as fences for such stolen property. One was Edward, a self-hiring slave who operated a dray with two mules and had possession of a stable on Seventh Street near Franklin; in May 1864 a municipal night watchman, acting on a tip, inspected the stable and found it crammed with bags of cornmeal and flour bearing the government's mark, along with quantities of sugar and whiskey of suspicious provenance. Among the more daring of the city's black thieves was Oliver, the servant of a government official, who used his access to Treasury Department facilities to make off with freshly printed sheets of Confederate currency; these he brought to a literate slave named Dick (a servant of President Davis, no less), who forged the necessary signatures on the bills.[40]

The urban environment not only offered slaves opportunities to make money but also permitted them considerable freedom of movement compared to rural slaves, most of whom were only occasionally allowed off their home farm or plantation. The combination of money and mobility helped sustain during the war, as before it, a vibrant, distinctively urban black subculture, some of it unconcealed and approved by whites, some of it underground and illicit. This subculture embraced free blacks as well as slaves.

Nearly all of the South's cities and many towns were home to one or more all-black churches. Black ministers and lay officials led these churches (which were mostly Baptist or Methodist, although the Christians, Episcopalians, and other denominations claimed a share). Nashville, for example, had four independent black churches by 1861, Savannah five, and Richmond six. Moreover, many of the white-controlled churches in the urban South sponsored separate services and other activities for their black members.[41]

Among the other urban institutions that brought blacks together were fire departments. Savannah's, for example, was nearly all black, comprising seven companies of slaves and two of free blacks, all officered by whites. One Savannah tradition that continued into the war years was the Firemen's Parade, held on the last Friday in May. This event began with a muster of the whole department and a formal inspection by the mayor and aldermen, following which the nine companies paraded through the city's streets in uniform, towing their engines (decorated like floats for the occasion) and singing marching songs while the populace cheered from the sidewalks. Another urban custom that continued during the war was the black charity ball, complete with orchestra and dancing. The Jackson, Mississippi, concert hall was the scene of one such gala on a Saturday night in October 1861; another was held in Augusta, Georgia, in May 1863, this one a costume ball with an admission fee of $10. A less formal urban institution, popular among the more prosperous blacks, was the Sunday promenade. In Jackson, Houston, and other cities, blacks dressed in fine clothes could be seen strolling or riding in cabs along the downtown streets on Sabbath afternoons (weather permitting), the men smoking cigars and the women wielding parasols.[42]

Coexisting with this public sphere of black urban culture was the late-night, clandestine world of black grogshops and gambling dens. These flourished despite municipal codes that forbade drinking, gambling, and unsupervised assembling by blacks and imposed on them a curfew. One such joint was located on the Plank Road on the outskirts of Montgomery, Alabama; there, in the winter of 1864–65, the slaves Pero, Sandy, Joel, Prince, Dick, and others would gather to drink whiskey and carouse into the wee hours.[43]

The relative freedom and affluence of urban slaves had long bothered many Southern whites. The wartime influx of slaves into the towns and cities, along with slaves' new opportunities for making money, aggravated that sense of grievance. White complaints about slaves in the urban Confederacy were loud and frequent. The editor of a Columbus, Georgia, newspaper decried in 1862 the late-night "passing to and fro of the negroes of this city."[44] A Houston editor, noting in 1863 the "unusually large number of slaves in our place owing to a variety of causes, and the liberties allowed them," claimed that they were growing "impudent, and impatient under restraint." He railed particularly against those who flaunted fancy dress and turned Sunday into a day of "noisy pastime and pleasure. Where do their get their money? Where the fine clothes [?]"[45] The Richmond *Examiner*'s editor was likewise outraged by "the spirit of extravagance, which [has] manifested itself among [blacks] since the war [began]. Negroes—slaves—buy delicacies in the markets that white people cannot afford; they ride in hacks, which white people cannot afford; and dress in raiment that nobody ought to afford [in] these wartimes."[46] Like many other whites, he was convinced that black thievery was funding this profligacy. "Wherein lies the panacea for this awful mania for stealing[?]," he asked in another editorial, in September 1864. "We think we have it. Hang a few upon conviction of burglary, and the evil spirits will depart out of the degenerate sons and daughters of Ham."[47]

Complaints of this sort provoked in many places heightened surveillance of slaves, and in some places thoroughgoing crackdowns. The mayor of Jackson proclaimed in March 1863 that the long-ignored city ordinances prohibiting slaves from living apart from their owners and "going at large, hiring their own time" would now be strictly enforced: "[T]he abuses . . . have become so great, and the demand for reform is so urgent, that the enforcement of the law can be no longer delayed."[48] The widow Garrett, who allowed her three slave men to violate similar ordinances in Canton, Mississippi, came to regret it. In 1862 the town authorities took note of the men's independent barbering and draying enterprises and slapped her with a $1,500 fine.[49] The Plank Road grogshop in Montgomery that catered to slaves was put out of business by a police raid in January 1865. Some of the patrons slipped away as the lawmen descended on the place, but five were caught and hauled before the city court. Found guilty of "unlawful assemblage," they were sentenced to 39 lashes apiece.[50]

Municipal courtrooms throughout the Confederacy were increasingly crowded with black offenders as the war went on. In Savannah the number of blacks appearing before the Mayor's Court on a typical day quintupled between late 1862 and late 1864.[51] In that city and elsewhere the usual punishment for municipal infractions by blacks was the whip. But in Richmond in October 1864 the slaves Ben and William, convicted in the Hustings Court of burglary, died on the gallows. The editor of the Richmond *Examiner*—who only a month before had urged just such a penalty for blacks guilty of that crime—noted that this was "the first instance of hanging for burglary within the jurisdiction of the courts of Richmond."[52]

Free blacks as well as slaves were targets of urban whites' suspicions, complaints, and crackdowns. More than 260,000 free blacks were living in the South when the

Civil War began. Of those, some 133,000 were in the 11 Confederate states, very unequally distributed: Virginia claimed 58,000 and North Carolina 30,000, but Florida, Mississippi, Arkansas, and Texas had fewer than 1,000 apiece. In the Upper South states, a large minority of free blacks (about one-third) lived in urban areas; in the Lower South states, a majority did so.[53]

Free blacks had an anomalous place in Southern society. Black but not enslaved, they generally held themselves to be above slaves in social status but were of course looked down on by whites. Enjoying some of the rights and privileges of free people (they could legally live on their own, claim compensation for their labor, own property, be a party to contracts, and so forth), they were denied others (they could not vote, hold office, or serve on juries; were subject to curfews and other restrictions; and could be whipped as punishment for crime). Most were unskilled, poor, and illiterate, but a significant minority boasted a skilled trade and comfortable circumstances, a good many could read and write, and a few enjoyed professional status (as ministers or businessmen) and real prosperity.[54]

Many Southern whites regarded free blacks as dangerous, a living denial of the beneficence of slavery and a bad influence on slaves. As white racial hysteria burgeoned in the months following Lincoln's election, they came under increased suspicion. Fearing what might come, some packed up their movable belongings, disposed of the rest, and emigrated to the North.[55] The outbreak of war posed further threats. In late April 1861, free blacks in Raleigh, North Carolina, were reported to be "alarmed for their personal safety."[56] Such fears were by no means irrational. As the war went on, free blacks in the Confederacy came under greater scrutiny and regulation. Georgia's legislature enacted laws forcing free blacks to register with local authorities and secure a white guardian who could guarantee their good behavior. That same body also considered (although it did not pass) a bill to enslave all free blacks and sell them off.[57]

As whites reined in the freedom of free blacks, they also put them to work for the Confederate cause. A south Mississippian, writing to a newspaper in July 1861, called attention to the free blacks in his section of the state, who he claimed were "rendering our country no service in time of need, [and are] a perfect nuisance, demoralizing to our slaves and causing much dissatisfaction."[58] His recommendation that they be put to work on fortifications was prescient; before long, state governments in the Confederacy were impressing free-black labor along with slave labor. Virginia did so beginning in February 1862, when the legislature declared all able-bodied free-black men ages 18 to 50 liable to impressment for up to 180 days. The Confederate government later followed suit. Thousands of free-black men were thus taken from their families during the war and sent off to the fortifications.[59]

Some free-black men fell victim to an informal sort of impressment. One was Isham Swett, a barber in Fayetteville, North Carolina. At the war's outbreak he voluntarily hired on as a body servant to a white soldier; but after four months he tired of the work, quit, returned home, and again took up his comb and shears. Local whites, how-ever, so vehemently criticized his abandonment of the army that by October 1861 he decided to return to it, citing "the pressure of public opinion."[60]

A few free blacks resisted such pressure, or tried to, and some likewise did their best to avoid impressment of the formal sort. In 1863 a literate man named Daniel Locklar, who lived in Laurinburg, North Carolina, petitioned the governor for protec-tion from an agent of the state salt works who was forcing Locklar and other free-black artisans to manufacture barrels for the works. "[He] Comes at the dead hours of night and carries us off wherever he thinks proper," Locklar wrote, "gives us one dollar and fifty Cents pr day and we [have to provide our own rations], I cannot support my fam-ily at that rate and pay the present high prices for provisions, . . . I can support my family very well if I were left at home to work for my neighbors. . . . [P]lease let me know if this Agent [has] *the power to use me as he does.*" Locklar's plea apparently suc-ceeded, for someone in the governor's office endorsed the petition, "He has no such authority."[61] In some cases whites who relied on the services of free-black artisans or laborers petitioned the authorities to exempt them from impressment.[62]

Other free-black men avoided impressment illegally. A justice of the peace in Farmville, Virginia, having received orders in 1863 to provide 52 free blacks from his county to work on fortifications and 10 others to work for the Niter and Mining bu-reau, replied that he could furnish no such number, in part because some of those sub-ject to such impressment calls were in the habit of fleeing their homes and hiding out whenever calls were announced. Other free-black men submitted to impressment but then slipped away as soon as they could. Of the 1,818 free-black Virginians impressed between February 1864 and March 1865, some 45 were eventually listed as deserters.[63]

A very few resisted violently. When an impressment officer in Petersburg, Virginia, came to a house in November 1863 and told the free-black man there that he must come with him, the man fled through a window in the back of the house, grabbing a musket on his way. The officer pursued him and fired his pistol, but missed, whereupon the flee-ing man stopped, turned, cursed and threatened the officer, aimed the musket at him, and pulled the trigger, only to have the weapon misfire. With that, the officer gave up the chase, and the man escaped. In the fall of 1861 a free-black man named Fletcher in Wilkesboro, North Carolina, refused the request of some local citizens to go off to the army as a body servant. When they insisted, he fled; accosted later by one of them, he pulled a pistol and shot the man to death. Fletcher was lodged in jail but did not live to face charges, for within two days a mob removed him by force and hanged him.[64]

While free blacks were generally unenthusiastic about laboring on fortifications or accompanying troops in the field, many gladly did war work of other sorts—when the terms were satisfactory. All the Confederate, state, and private facilities and agencies that hired slaves also hired free blacks, especially the skilled. The Tredegar Iron Works employed large numbers at good wages, as did the railroads. The 13 free-black firemen and train hands working for the Petersburg Railroad in early 1862, for example, made an average of $19 a month. The hospitals were another source of good jobs. At the army's Charlottesville General Hospital a free-black married couple, Patsy and Robert Goings, together earned $25 per month along with meals and lodging, she as a laundress and he as a nurse. Patsy thus continued doing the sort of work she had done before the war (the 1860 census listed her as a washerwoman); but for Robert (a carpenter by trade) this was a new endeavor—one not as lucrative as carpentry, but which did exempt him from impressment.[65]

Other free blacks who took well-paying jobs included Richmonders John Gordon and George Sprills, who hired on with the Quartermaster bureau as ship carpenters at $100 a month. Some did even better. At the Quartermaster facility in Richmond where army ambulances were manufactured and repaired, 11 of the 55 hired artisans were free blacks, including several blacksmiths, some sawyers, a carpenter, and a painter; these men earned as much as $5 a day. Some free blacks declined to take new employment but nevertheless profited from the war. One was James Muschett, who owned a general store in Quantico Mills, Virginia. Among his wartime customers were Confederate soldiers posted in the vicinity, to whom he sold tobacco, liquor, groceries, and dry goods.[66]

As they toiled, and in many cases prospered, in the wartime Confederacy, urban blacks sought to allay the suspicions of whites and protect themselves from reprisals. One way to do this was to act as deferential and unthreatening as possible in the presence of whites. Another was to display devotion to the Confederacy.

In the war's first months a considerable number of free blacks publicly proclaimed their support for the Rebel cause and volunteered their services. The New Orleans Native Guards and other free-black militia companies have already been mentioned. Among the other self-proclaimed free-black patriots were 60 Savannah men who tendered their labor to the government in April 1861, 350 Virginia men who volunteered that same month to work on the Norfolk fortifications, and a number of Savannah women who in June busied themselves sewing uniforms for the troops, having pledged to make 100. While the enthusiasm for voluntary military labor soon evaporated, other manifestations of free-black patriotism continued through the war. Savannah's free blacks were particularly demonstrative: some gave money to provide winter clothing for Confederate soldiers serving in Virginia, others donated food to a local charitable hospital for soldiers, and still others subscribed to the Gunboat Fund, which was established to support the construction of a warship to defend the city.[67]

Some urban slaves, too, publicly avowed Rebel loyalty. In April 1861 they gathered in the streets of Columbia, Greenville, and other South Carolina cities and towns to cheer the news of Fort Sumter's surrender. Donations for various patriotic purposes came from slaves throughout the Confederacy, such as the $3.95 that the black members of the Methodist church of Camden, South Carolina, contributed in 1862 for the benefit of sick and wounded soldiers and the 25 cents that Mary and Alexander of

Savannah each gave to the Gunboat Fund that same year.[68] The wartime black charity balls, in many or most cases, benefited military hospitals, soldiers' aid societies, and the like. The one in Jackson, Mississippi, in October 1861—dubbed by its sponsors the "Confederate Ball"—raised $45, after deducting expenses, for the town's Ladies Aid Association. "We tender it," said a literate black man in a letter enclosing the donation, "as an evidence of sympathy for our masters who have gone forth to fight for the institution [i.e., slavery] which affords us so much protection and happiness."[69]

Such patriotic words and deeds were touted by whites as evidence of the essential harmony of the South's biracial, hierarchical society and the manifest justness of the Confederate cause (although, as pointed out in chapter 1, more often than not such white affirmations masked profound private fears about blacks). An Abbeville, South Carolina, newspaper editor, describing the jubilation of blacks when Fort Sumter surrendered, declared that "There is to-day more . . . good feeling, more contentment, among our negroes than at any period of our history. So much for abolitionism, and its efforts to create a servile war."[70] A Savannah editor, noting the many slaves and free blacks who donated money for soldiers' winter clothing, cited the fact as "another of the thousand instances which go to prove the interest our colored population feel in driving back the thieving vandals from our soil."[71]

Certainly there were slaves who were content enough with their lot, or who identified closely enough with their master, that they sincerely supported the Confederate cause; the body servants who endured the hardships of military service while ignoring opportunities to escape are examples. And no doubt an even larger proportion of free blacks—who enjoyed a comparatively privileged existence—truly supported the Rebels' struggle to preserve the Old South's way of life. But the vast majority of black professions of Confederate patriotism were differently motivated.

Compassion alone probably accounts for most black donations to military hospitals and soldiers' aid societies, for the suffering of fellow human beings touched the hearts of blacks no less than the hearts of whites. A different impulse prompted most of the cheering over Fort Sumter's surrender, the donations to the Gunboat Fund, and other black gestures celebrating or promoting Confederate military victory. These were calculated acts of self-protection, intended to curry favor with the dominant race and thus forestall white suspicion and ward off the intensified racial repression encouraged by the outbreak of war.[72]

A free-black New Orleans man, explaining to Union authorities in 1863 why he and hundreds of his fellows had joined the Native Guards in 1861 and offered their services to the Confederacy, put it this way: "[W]e could not help it. If we had not volunteered, they would have forced us into the ranks, and we should have been suspected. We have property and rights here, and there is every reason why we should take care of ourselves." There was hardly an authentic Rebel among the Native Guards, he said: "[T]here are not five men in the regiment [who support] the Confederacy."[73] Lest his statement be dismissed as simply currying favor with new masters, it should be kept in mind that the Native Guards were under no compulsion when they volunteered for the Union cause after New Orleans was captured, and thereafter served and died in that cause.

While free blacks and slaves alike were subjugated in the Civil War South, the fundamental fact that free blacks were not property protected them in important ways. For one thing, they were not separated from their loved ones by sale. They were exempt, too, from forced removal. During the war many slaveowners, fearful for the security of their human property, moved that property to safer areas. Exactly how many slaves were thus taken from their homes is indeterminable, but they numbered probably not just in the tens of thousands but the hundreds of thousands.[74]

The desire to keep valuable property from the clutches of Yankee invaders prompted the great majority of slave removals during the sectional crisis. But removals actually began before military invasion, and even before the war. In January 1861 a South Carolina planter who opposed secession abandoned his state and moved with his 60 slaves to a Southern state still in the Union; other Unionists in the seceding states did the same that winter. As the crisis unfolded, some masters of the other political persuasion took their slaves in the opposite direction. These included a number of Marylanders who protested their state's Unionist stance by resettling in Alabama in the spring of 1861, and some Kentuckians who protested their state's neutrality by heading south in August.[75]

In areas occupied by Union military forces, both in seceding and nonseceding Southern states, masters took away slaves in great numbers—even in the early part of the war, when federal authorities disavowed any intention of meddling with slavery. Many Missouri slaves, for example, were being taken south by the fall of 1861. The Union amphibious operations that seized offshore islands and coastal enclaves of Florida, Georgia, South Carolina, North Carolina, and Virginia in 1861 and 1862 provoked extensive removals inland. The invasions of northern Virginia, middle and west Tennessee, and northern Alabama in the first part of 1862 drove many masters southward with their slaves; the seizure of the upper and lower sections of the Mississippi River in those months drove many others eastward or westward. Slave removals multiplied beginning in the fall of 1862, when federal policy shifted toward emancipation. Union capture of the remainder of the Mississippi River in mid-1863 and the invasion of Georgia in 1864 generated great waves of slave relocation. When masters in threatened regions hesitated to move, Confederate military authorities often encouraged or ordered them to do so, lest the slaves end up as laborers or soldiers in the Union army.[76]

Sometimes removal took slaves no great distance from home. In the coastal Georgia county of Liberty, for example, some slaveowners moved no farther than the county's upper reaches, just far enough to avoid the Yankees who prowled the coast in steamboats and came ashore in raiding parties. But most slaves who were removed had to travel much farther, sometimes many hundreds of miles. One was a young girl named Milly who lived on a plantation in Mississippi. In the spring of 1864 her master called his slaves together to announce that he intended to keep them well beyond the grasp of the Yankees; prepare to move, he commanded. Two days later they began the long trek to their new home in North Carolina.[77]

Some slaves were taken away by rail, some by steamboat. But most went by road, on foot or in wagons, traveling by day, camping by night, and cooking meals over open fires. Milly was one of many who retained, into old age, vivid memories of wartime relocation by wagon train. Another was Allen Manning, who was about 12 in 1862, when his master moved him, his parents, his siblings, and all the other hands from their Mississippi plantation home to a place in Louisiana. Five wagons carried the provisions and the very youngest and oldest slaves; the other slaves, including Allen, trudged along beside the wagons—although once, when Allen sickened from overexposure to the sun, he was allowed to ride. The arrival of these slaves in Louisiana did not end their odyssey, however. The very next year, worried by further Yankee incursions, Allen's master ordered the slaves to load up the wagons and then led them off to a new home in Texas. On this trek, Allen's mother gave birth on the road, to a girl; the master decreed that the newborn would be named Texana.[78]

A few slaves experienced removal as something of a frolic. When 46 men, women, and children belonging to planter Isaac Erwin abandoned their Iberville Parish, Louisiana, home at Christmastime 1862 and headed to Texas by wagon train, Erwin noted that they were "Dancing every Night and very Merry."[79] But for most there was no joy in being thus uprooted and led away to a strange place. For one thing, many removals were not planned well in advance and carried out unhurriedly, as was that of the Erwin slaves, but were instead sudden and frantic. Elderly ex-slave Elvira Boles, born about 1842, recalled her experience in the last year of the war, when her master abruptly ordered his slaves to leave their Holmes County, Mississippi, plantation home and go by wagon to Texas. "Marster said dey was runnin' us from de Yankees to keep us. . . . 'You ain't got no time to take nothin' to whar you goin' [he said]. Take your little bundle and leave all you has in your house.'" Until these slaves got a good distance away, their journey was a nightmare of anxiety and forced marches: "We was a dodgin' in and out, runnin' from de Yankees. . . . [Master] tol' us de Yankees 'ud kill us iffen dey foun' us." Elvira arrived in Texas with no dress besides the one she was wearing, and without the child with whom she had begun the journey: "I lost my baby, its buried somewhere on dat road. Died at Red River and we left it."[80]

The agony of removal was often compounded by the separation of families. Some refugee slaveowners brought away only a portion of their slaves, leaving the rest; and even when all the slaves went together, many left behind loved ones owned by other masters. The cold calculus of profit generally determined which slaves a master took and which he left. Older slaves, past their most productive working years, were frequently left behind; sometimes only the able-bodied men were taken away, leaving the women, children, and elderly men.[81] Milly's master made fateful choices as his slaves loaded the wagons for the journey to North Carolina in 1864: "He picks me out," Milly recalled, "but my gran'maw he sez dat he will leave case she am so old an' feeble." Milly was devastated, for her grandmother was her closest family member on the plantation.[82] Other slaveowners severed even more intimate bonds. A married couple named Minerva and Anderson were separated when their master took Anderson off to South Carolina. Slaveowner Thomas Steward of Mississippi took at least one of his slave women from her children, sending her to Arkansas.[83]

Resistance, in the form of running away, flared up on occasion when removal threatened. In the spring of 1863, upon learning that they would soon be taken away to South Carolina, 14 slaves of a Tippah County, Mississippi, master—nearly all he owned—disappeared overnight. Others who were determined not to be dragged away from their home waited until their journey had begun and then slipped away at the first opportunity along the road. Masters who anticipated such trouble took precautions. A former slave named Adeline, who as a girl had belonged to the Jones family of Bolivar County, Mississippi, recalled that when she and the other Jones slaves were removed eastward by wagon train those deemed likely to try to escape were chained at night, their legs securely fastened to a tree or wagon wheel.[84]

Most removed slaves were plantation hands who, on arriving at their destination, resumed the sort of work they were familiar with. Many refugee masters secured a new plantation before moving, thus affording themselves and their laborers a relatively smooth transition. Such was the case of a lowcountry South Carolina planter who in 1862 moved his 156 slaves inland some 250 miles to a plantation he had recently purchased. This 856-acre place was long established and fully equipped with buildings, fencing, farm implements, hogs, and cattle, as well as new crops of corn and cotton already in the ground. As soon as the hands arrived they moved into the slave quarters and set to work in the fields. (The only hitch in this process was that the previous planter had had fewer slaves, and so there were not enough cabins in the quarters; some of the new arrivals had to be housed temporarily in tents.) Other removed slaves, however, particularly many who went to the Texas frontier, had to break virgin ground and build a plantation from scratch.[85]

Some planters, unable or unwilling to resume planting, hired out their slaves after relocating them. While many such slaves ended up on farms or plantations, many others went to war-related industrial establishments or other nonagricultural workplaces. Niger, a house servant on a plantation in Liberty County on the Georgia coast, was among the latter. In early 1864 he was sent to Atlanta, where some relatives of his owner lived. They found work for him in a tannery a mile from their house. There his tasks included chopping firewood and hauling tanbark, for which his owner received $33 a month and he received clothing and board. He lodged not at the tannery but with his owner's relatives, along with his wife, Tenah, and baby, Cinda. Niger came to like his new situation for the most part, for the work was not particularly hard and his employer was a decent man, but he was disappointed that no overtime system was in place by which he might earn money of his own.[86]

Niger was among the fortunate removed slaves, for he stayed with his wife and child and ended up in tolerable circumstances. Among the many unfortunates were the thousands whose destination turned out to be the auction block. A good many refugee masters, short of cash or needing fewer laborers because of their new situation, sold off some or all of their slaves. A Richmond newspaper reported in October 1862 that so many of the slaves removed from northern Virginia counties had been put on the market in Richmond that prices were depressed; the editor urged refugees to send their slaves to markets farther south, and no doubt many followed that advice.[87] Young Adeline of Bolivar County, Mississippi, who saw some of her fellow slaves chained up during their removal, witnessed more horrors before her odyssey ended, for she and all the others were sold off along their route—with no regard for family ties. "Some of us was sold to people in Demopolis, Alabama, an' Atlanta, Georgia," she recalled in old age, "an' some to folks in Meridian and Shubuta, Mississippi." Adeline ended up as a house girl in Shubuta. She never saw any of her family again.[88]

Adeline remained a slave until after the Civil War ended, as did most other Southerners who were unfree when it began. A great number, however, celebrated their release from bondage before the Rebel armies capitulated. They followed various paths to freedom. Chapter 4 examines the multiplicity of ways in which black liberation came to the wartime South.

Blacks representing several generations on a South Carolina plantation, 1862. Slaves endeavored to keep their family ties intact despite the disruptions of war. (Courtesy of the Library of Congress)

Preparing cotton for ginning on a South Carolina plantation, 1862. Most slaves in the wartime South continued to work on farms and plantations, as they had before the war. (Courtesy of the Library of Congress)

A business establishment where slaves were bought and sold, Atlanta, Georgia, 1864. The selling of slaves continued unabated in the Confederate states until the war's end. (Courtesy of the Library of Congress)

Tredegar Iron Works, Richmond, Virginia, April 1865. Many thousands of slaves and free blacks in the Confederacy worked in industrial establishments like this one during the war, making arms, ammunition, and equipment for the Rebel army. (Courtesy of the Library of Congress)

First African Church, Richmond, Virginia, spring 1865. Urban slaves and free blacks in the South, before and during the war, enjoyed a measure of independence denied those in the rural areas; many worshipped in independent black churches like this one. (Courtesy of the Library of Congress)

Runaway slaves, just arrived in Union army lines, probably in Virginia, January 1, 1863. President Lincoln signed the Emancipation Proclamation that very day, committing the U.S. government and army to upholding the freedom of black people such as these. (Courtesy of the Library of Congress)

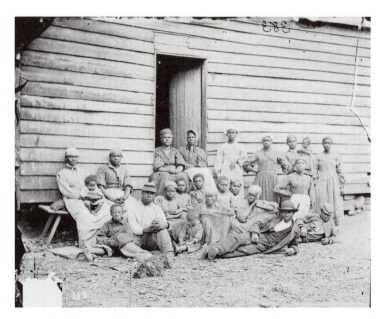

"Contrabands," Cumberland Landing, Virginia, May 1862. The legal status of the fugitive slaves pictured here was uncertain; although they were within Union army lines and no longer under their master's control, the U.S. government had not yet declared the slaves free. (Courtesy of the Library of Congress)

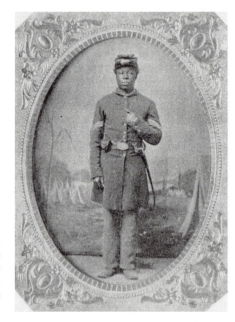

A Southern black man in Union army uniform. This is Sergeant William Bronson of the 1st South Carolina Infantry (later called the 33rd U.S. Colored Infantry), one of 141,000 Southern blacks who served in ranks of the Union army.

Union army teamsters, Bermuda Hundred, Virginia, 1864. Thousands of blacks who gained freedom in the invaded regions of the South went to work for the U.S. army, and some such as these accompanied forces in the field; many thousands of others, still enslaved, did so for the Confederate army. (Courtesy of the Library of Congress)

Black Union troops skirmish with Confederates on the Georgia coast, November 1862. Black combat troops like these contributed greatly to Union military victory, as did black troops who performed noncombat roles such as manning fortifications, garrisoning captured towns, and guarding transportation lines.

FOUR

GAINING FREEDOM

Hundreds of thousands of enslaved people became free before the Civil War ended. Many gained freedom through their own daring and cunning, combined with a measure of luck and assistance from the Yankees; others did so purely through the force of Union arms. Still others were freed by state or federal legal action, and some were simply abandoned or cast out by their masters.

The major force driving wartime emancipation, besides the slaves' fervent desire to be free, was the transformation of Union policy toward the rebellious Southern states, a tidal shift away from conciliation and conservatism to coercion and revolution. This shift was prompted in part by strategic considerations. The stunning successes of the Confederate army in the eastern theater in 1861 and 1862 demonstrated that Union victory in the war was not assured and encouraged the use of all available means to defeat the Rebels—including depriving them of their valuable slave labor. President Lincoln and other federal officials also recognized that emancipation would be applauded by most Europeans and thus hurt the Confederacy's chances for foreign recognition and aid.

As the strategic benefits of emancipation were becoming apparent, some of the political obstacles to it were disappearing. It gradually became clear to federal policy makers and soldiers in the field that most white people in the seceded states were diehard Rebels who were not going to be coaxed back to the Union no matter how gently they were treated or how earnestly their peculiar institution was safeguarded by the Yankee invaders. Harsher measures toward them would, therefore, make national reunification no more difficult than it already was. And, too, by 1862 the Border states were under firm enough Union military control that the government could move against slavery with no fear that those states would respond by seceding. Questions about the legality of emancipation could be answered by defining it as a war measure— useful in weakening the Confederate military effort, and no different in principle from destroying Rebel railroads and munitions factories.

By the late summer of 1862 these facts had persuaded President Lincoln and many other Northerners that emancipation would be strategically profitable, politically feasible, and legally justifiable. But whether it was a practical possibility was another matter.

Two things combined to make it a practical possibility: the presence of Union armies in the South and the slaves' thirst for freedom. Neither alone could have made emancipation an achievable aim; both were essential. Obviously, if no Union forces were on hand to challenge the slaveholders' power and harbor black fugitives, few slaves would benefit from a policy of emancipation. But if the enslaved men and women of the South were as content in their servitude and as loyal to their masters as many Southern whites insisted they were, an emancipation policy would likewise be fruitless, for the Union invaders would have to drag slaves away from their masters at gunpoint and keep them under constant guard to prevent them from running back. This would require diverting troops from the front lines in such numbers as to compromise the Union military effort and thus negate the benefits of depriving the Rebels of their slave labor. Moreover, the slaves' willingness not only to desert their masters but also to aid the Union armies (as workers and soldiers, discussed in chapter 5) meant that each laboring black person who was freed would be not just one less asset for the Confederacy but also one more for the Union. When federal policy makers weighed the potential costs and benefits of emancipation, the aspirations and convictions and deeds of the slaves tipped the balance. The enslaved people of the South were essential agents in moving the U.S. government toward the momentous decision to make war on slavery.

A series of legislative acts and presidential proclamations marked the government's movement to emancipation. In August 1861, after a number of slaves employed in constructing fortifications (or otherwise directly supporting the Rebel armies) had fled to the Union lines, Congress passed a Confiscation Act that forbade the return of such slaves, although it did not technically free them. A March 1862 law decreed that no Union troops could be used to return any enslaved runaway; this did not, however, prevent masters from retrieving their runaways from the Union lines. A second Confiscation Act, passed in July 1862, declared free all slaves owned by secessionists; it was not really the decisive measure that it might seem, however, for it left it up to federal courts ultimately to decide which masters and slaves were affected. President Lincoln dispelled the ambiguities of federal policy in September 1862, when he issued the preliminary Emancipation Proclamation. This announced that all slaves in areas still in rebellion on January 1, 1863, would on that day be deemed free.

The President's final Emancipation Proclamation on New Year's Day was a legalistic document that explicitly justified itself as an exercise of presidential war power and spelled out precisely which areas were affected. The nonseceding Southern states (including the soon-to-be state of West Virginia) were exempted, as were sections of the Confederacy where U.S. military forces were in place and where some of the citizens had taken steps to bring their states back into the Union: 6 counties in eastern Virginia, 13 parishes in southeastern Louisiana, and the whole state of Tennessee. The Proclamation's stiff prose and many exceptions did not, however, obscure its profound meaning. Although it had no immediate practical effect on the enslaved people in territory currently under Confederate control, it did affect those in many Rebel areas currently under Union control and would affect those in all Rebel areas that came under Union control in the future. And it served notice to every soldier in the field that liberating slaves was now his sworn duty.[1]

While the U.S. government inched toward de jure emancipation in 1861 and 1862, a good number of Union soldiers and Southern slaves were carrying out their own policy of de facto emancipation. Some of the soldiers involved were abolitionists who seized the opportunity of military service to give substance to their hatred of slavery and their sympathy for the enslaved. Others were expressing contempt for the rebellious white Southerners who owned the slaves. Still others were acting out of gratitude for the slaves' help, for black men and women in the invaded regions often gave the Yankees useful information about the location of enemy forces, advantageous routes of march, and so forth.[2] "The white people are treacherous and unreliable," reported a federal officer in middle Tennessee in March 1862, "all lying to deceive us. We can only depend on the statements of the negroes."[3] A Union general in northern Alabama that spring concurred: "The negroes are our only friends, and in two instances I owe my own safety to their faithfulness. . . . [A]ll who communicate to me valuable information I have promised the protection of my Government."[4]

Whatever motivated the Union troops involved, some slaves in the occupied South found sanctuary and freedom in the federal army camps well before President Lincoln put his pen to the Emancipation Proclamation. Such instances encouraged other slaves to slip away from their owners and try their luck with the invaders. Many were rebuffed (as noted in chapter 1), but as time passed more and more were rewarded for their boldness. A Union officer in middle Tennessee in March 1862 remarked disingenuously that black runaways were coming into the lines in considerable numbers "and in some mysterious way are so disposed of that their masters never hear of them again."[5] Fugitives also found haven in Fredericksburg, Virginia, after Union forces captured the town that spring. "Matters are getting worse and worse here every day with regard to the negroes," wrote a white resident in mid-May. "They are leaving their owners by the hundred." A few weeks later she reported that "Runaway negroes from the country around continue to come in every day. . . . [There are] men, women, little children and babies coming in in gangs of ten and twenty at a time."[6] In late July a west Tennessee planter decried the breakdown of slavery in that region and railed against the Yankee occupiers' refusal to preserve the institution: "General insurbordination amongst our slave population. . . . No arrangements can be made for the delivery of fugitives."[7] Three weeks later another west Tennessee planter echoed that complaint: "Negroes have every thing in their own hands and they know it, surrounded and protected as they are by Federal soldiers. As many as see proper can walk off & there is *no remedy*." In mid-November he observed disgustedly that "The Federal camps are swarming with negroes."[8]

In sections of the Confederacy invaded and held after January 1, 1863, slavery died abruptly. Indeed, hammered by the mighty combination of the slaves' desire to be free, the Union army's presence, and the Emancipation Proclamation's mandate, the peculiar institution in some places did not just expire but exploded. Alfred Quine, overseer of Fonsylvania plantation near Vicksburg, Mississippi, recorded in his diary what happened when General Ulysses S. Grant's army occupied the area in the spring of 1863. Reports of the Yankees' approach reached the plantation as early as May 6, causing "grate exsitement" among the hands but not seriously disrupting work on the place. Grant's troops closed in around Vicksburg on May 19, but none appeared for the time being at Fonsylania and the hands labored on in the fields under Quine's direction. The overseer noted, however, the increasing tension in the air. The tension broke suddenly on the 25th: "All hands went to work and worked up to 12 oclock," Quine wrote that day, "and [then] the yankees came and set the Negros all Free and the work all stoped." His subsequent entries vividly document the obliteration of slavery in that little corner of the South. May 26: "Negros all Free no work dun." May 27: "Negros doing nothing & yankees came here to day and took 2 waggon Loads of corn[.] Saulsbery Daniel Little John and Henry [slaves] with waggon & oxen went with the yankees." May 28: "Negros doing nothing." May 29: "Negros All doing nothing. . . . George Richard & Jo went to the yankees to day." May 31: "[Y]ankees came to day and took 5 oxen and 25 sheep[.] Ned went to the Yankees." June 1: "Negros all riding about and doing nothing." June 2: "Elic gaither Jim & Bose went to the yankees to day[.] All the rest doing nothing." June 3: "Negros All doing nothing[.] from 2 to 5 Yankees here evry day." June 5: "Negros All frolican." June 6: "[H]oliday all the time now with the Negros."[9]

The exemptions stipulated in the Emancipation Proclamation quickly became meaningless, at least with regard to the seceded states. After January 1, 1863, Union troops in the field generally treated all Confederate territory as subject to emancipation, and their superiors made little or no effort to enforce the exemptions. A Nashville slaveowner was made aware of the true state of affairs after he tracked down one of his runaway slaves in July 1863 and took her back home by force; soldiers of the Union garrison's provost guard soon appeared, released the woman, arrested her master, and took him before the provost marshal, who told him firmly that "*the time [has] passed when negroes [can] be whipped in this country.*"[10] A Union general in Nashville summed up the situation in January 1864: "Slavery is virtually dead in Tennessee, although the State is excepted from the emancipation proclamation. Negroes leave their homes and stroll over the country uncontrolled. . . . In many cases negroes . . . [go to] work for themselves, [while still] boarding and lodging with their masters, defiantly asserting their right to do it. . . . [Troops] go [in]to the country[side] and bring in wagon loads of negro women and children to this city, and I suppose to other posts."[11] Another Union officer in Tennessee around that time affirmed that the army's de facto policy there was to "keep all [the slaves] we get, and get all we can."[12] Legal emancipation came to the Volunteer State in early 1865, when a newly created Unionist state government amended the state constitution to abolish slavery. Slavery was similarly extinguished in the exempted counties and parishes of Virginia and Louisiana before the war's end.[13]

Some slaves in occupied areas gained freedom not because they seized it or because the Yankees demanded it but because their owner ceded it to them. Refugee masters, as noted in chapter 3, often left behind their less productive slaves—women with infants, old people, the infirm—while taking the rest away. And in some cases Yankee invasion came with so little warning that fleeing masters were forced to abandon all or nearly all their slaves, of whatever sex or age or condition. Such was the case on the Sea Islands of the south Atlantic coast, which fell quite suddenly to a Union amphibious force in the fall of 1861, leaving thousands of black people masterless.[14]

In occupied districts where slavery was still technically in force but clearly unraveling, some slaves had freedom thrust on them by frustrated masters. A Union officer commanding a post in southeastern Louisiana observed in June 1862 "a large number of Negroes, of both sexes and all ages, who are lying near our pickets, with bag and baggage. . . . Many of these Negroes have been sent away from one of the neighboring sugar plantations, by their owner, . . . who tells them, I am informed, that 'the Yankees are King here now, and that they must go to their King for food and shelter.'"[15] A white woman in the occupied town of Athens, Alabama, told of an incident in August 1862 at a plantation near the town: "Jimmy Coman had a fuss with the negroes last week . . . and ended with driving Merritt (the best one they've got) off, telling him if he ever came back there . . . he'd shoot him, so he's with the Yankees."[16] In middle Tennessee in 1863, according to a federal soldier, great numbers of slaves "have been abandoned by their masters, who have lost all hope of gain by keeping them and now cruelly turn them out to perish or to become a burden [to our] army."[17]

While all enslaved people in Union-controlled Confederate territory eventually gained freedom one way or another, it must be kept in mind that such territory was but a small portion of the Confederate South before the summer of 1865, and that until then the black people who resided in such territory were but a small minority of those in the seceded states (a minority rendered even smaller by the forced removal of many before the Yankees arrived, as discussed in chapter 3). For the great majority of Confederate slaves through the spring of 1865, Union invasion and the policy of emancipation offered only the possibility, not the certainty, of freedom. And yet tens of thousands of those residing outside the spheres of Union control realized that possibility.

Some of those tens of thousands could thank the fortuitous appearance of a Yankee raiding party. Throughout the war, Union forces raided Confederate-controlled areas to destroy railroads and other things of military value or to gather provisions for their own use. After 1862, the raiders often brought slaves back with them. A Mississippi slaveowner described in March 1863 the recent visit of a party of "Yankee scoundrels" to his neighborhood: they seized chickens, hogs, sheep, cattle, mules, and horses, and when they departed they were followed by dozens of slaves who had decided that this was the day of Jubilee.[18] In another part of Mississippi later that spring, a sizeable force of raiders passed through; after torching vast quantities of stored corn, bacon, and cotton and every grist-mill they found, they returned to their post with a thousand head of cattle, hundreds of horses and mules, and, as their commander boasted in his report, "an army of negroes, nearly equal to the number of men in my command."[19] The destructive march of General William T. Sherman's army from Atlanta to Savannah in late 1864 and then northward through the Carolinas in early 1865 was essentially a gigantic raid that gave many slaves the opportunity to desert their master (although Sherman never encouraged them to do so, regarding such fugitives as a burden). By the time the army reached Cumberland County, North Carolina, in mid-March 1865, the number of slaves following it had reached 7,000.[20]

Those 7,000 and others like them had obviously paid no heed to the horror stories spread by masters about the diabolical Yankees. "White folks tole us you burned [black] men in the[ir] houses & drowned the women & children," a slave man told one of Sherman's officers during the march from Atlanta to Savannah. "Well," the officer responded, "did you believe it?" "No, *Sir*!!," was the reply. "We didn't believe it—*we has faith in you!*" Recounting this incident in his diary, the officer added that "It is amusing to see how desperately the rebs have been lying to their slaves about us, & what a failure it is. The darkies receive it all very gravely, & then run away & join us & tell us about it, & beg to go along with [us]."[21]

As noted in chapter 1, not all the slaves who encountered Yankee raiders willing to take them were willing to go. In a few cases, the unwilling were taken by force. A white girl living on a large Mississippi plantation described the visit of a raiding party in April 1863. On arriving, the soldiers told the slaves that they intended to "take the last one of them whether they wanted to go or not." They subsequently rounded up all the slaves, "some of them at the point of the bayonet, for some refused to come with them at first." They marched away with 160 black people, not all of whom hailed their emancipation as a blessing.[22]

Slaves in the Confederate South who sought freedom but were not lucky enough to be in areas occupied or raided by the Yankees had to get to the Union lines on their own. Such flight was enormously risky, however, for, as discussed in chapter 1, whites vigilantly guarded against escapes and often brutally punished captured fugitives. So fierce was the desire for freedom, however, that many blacks accepted the risk, and some were successful.

Certain slaves were more likely than others to make the attempt. Those living within a few days' travel of the Union lines were far likelier to try than those farther away, for the odds of being spotted and apprehended by wary whites increased substantially with every mile traversed. But some slaves who resided in regions distant from the Yankees were brought closer by the circumstances of war and managed to exploit that opportunity. Numbers of those impressed to work on Rebel fortifications slipped away from their guards and through the picket lines and reached the protection of federal forces. The Union navy's blockading vessels offered a haven for some of the slaves engaged in salt-making or other work on the seacoast. Among them were eight men employed by the Lee County Salt Company on Florida's Gulf coast. They were at work in September 1862 when a rowboat manned by a squad of sailors from a blockading ship approached the shore, on a mission to secure firewood and drinking water. The slaves' white supervisor ordered them to follow him as he headed inland for safety; they refused, went off to hail the sailors and greet them on the beach, and were subsequently taken aboard the rowboat and brought out to the ship.[23]

A good number of Rebel army officers' body servants likewise took advantage of their proximity to the Yankees to gain freedom—to the chagrin of their masters, who thought them the most loyal of slaves.[24] One was Abram, the South Carolina boy mentioned in chapter 3 who served his owner, Major James Griffin, on the Virginia front and impressed him as a resourceful forager. In a May 1862 letter to his wife, Griffin reported Abram's desertion and confessed his own puzzlement: "I fear I have lost Abram. He left me while I was at Yorktown, and I havent heard a word from him since. It is very singular and I cant account for it. He has been a good boy and a faithful one to me most of the time, since I have been in service. . . . He left me on the 28th of April[.] He went out as usual to buy provisions, and got a pass to cross the York river. . . . This is the last I heard of him."[25]

Other factors that often influenced a slave's decision to attempt escape included age, sex, and family ties. The most likely to try were unmarried young men or boys like Abram; the least likely were the elderly and women with small children. And yet there were some of the latter sorts who dared to flee, doing so sometimes in family groups.[26] A former slave named J. T. Tims recalled his family's escape from a plantation in Jefferson

County, Mississippi, during the latter part of the war, when Tims was around 11 years old. He and his parents and siblings were among 12 slaves who slipped away from the plantation one Sunday night, heading northwest toward the Mississippi River, 20 miles away, with the hope of flagging down a passing U.S. navy gunboat. They did make contact with a vessel, but when the crew refused to take them aboard the fugitives had to resume their journey, heading southward along the river toward the Yankee-occupied town of Natchez, 30 or more miles distant. "We went there walking and wading," as Tims remembered, traveling no doubt by night and hiding in the woods by day. The trek was long and dangerous, but luck was with them. "We was from Sunday night to Sunday night gettin' there. We didn't have no trouble 'cept that the hounds was runnin' us. But they didn't catch us. . . . [W]e all got to Natchez."[27]

Some escapes were long in the planning while others came on the spur of the moment. Among the fugitives whose flight was long contemplated was a young man named Allen Parker of Chowan County in eastern North Carolina. By the summer of 1862 Yankee gunboats were prowling the nearby Chowan River, encouraging Parker and his fellow slaves to think of escape. "[A]s the summer months passed," he recalled in his memoir, "[we] felt more and more restless." Despite the increased watchfulness of local whites, he was able to meet furtively with other slaves in the neighborhood to discuss "the doings of the 'Yankees' . . . and ideas in rela[t]ion to freedom." As the summer wore on, they made more definite plans.[28]

Parker made his break for freedom one night in August, along with three friends. "We waited till everything was quiet . . . and then stole our way down to the river bank, where we knew there was a boat." This boat, which was simply a dugout cypress canoe, was chained to a tree, but Parker managed to pry it loose. Then away the four men paddled, toward the reported location of a gunboat. They found it not far away; but their freedom was by no means assured, for emancipation had not yet been officially proclaimed. As they hopefully approached the vessel they were hailed by an officer on board. They told him they were runaways seeking refuge, adding that they would like to know right away if they would receive sanctuary, for if not they would have to hurry back to their homes before their absence was noticed at sunup. The officer asked if their owners were Unionists; no, the slaves replied, they were secessionists. He then disappeared, while they waited nervously in the canoe. "When the officer came back he said he had orders from the captain to let us come aboard. We immediately accepted the invitation, and being very tired, were soon fast asleep on the deck of the vessel." Parker and his friends awoke in the morning to begin their first day as free men.[29]

Other escapes were impromptu events, sparked by some troubling incident or news and involving a slave who might otherwise have remained obediently at home. The threat of being sold away or removed to a distant place provoked some to flee to the Yankees.[30] So did the threat of forced labor on Rebel fortifications. Late in 1864 a white resident of Madison County, Virginia, which lay close to the federal lines, begged the state's governor to exempt the county from the recent call for laborers, pointing out that many slaves would simply not submit to it: "Numbers of them say, that while they have no disposition to leave, yet before they will go to Richmond, during the winter season, to work on the fortifications . . . they will go to the yankees."[31]

Severe punishment or the threat of it likewise spurred enslaved people to abandon their homes. An elderly ex-slave named Boston Blackwell recalled for an interviewer the circumstances that provoked his abrupt flight, in October 1863 at age 15, from the Arkansas plantation where he lived to the Union-occupied town of Pine Bluff:

> They was building a new house [on the plantation]; I wanted to feel some putty in my hand. One early morning I clim a ladder to get a little chunk and the overseer man, he seed me. Here he come, yelling [at] me to get down; he gwine whip me 'cause I'se a thief, he say. He call a slave boy and tell him cut ten [willow] whips; he gwine wear every one out on me. When he's gone to eat breakfas', I runs to my cabin and tells my sister, "I'se leaving this here place for good." She cry and say, "Overseer man, he kill you." I says, "He kill me anyhow." The young boy what cut the whips—he named Jerry—he come along wif me, and we wade the stream for long piece. Heerd the hounds a-howling, getting ready for to chase after us. Then we hide in dark woods. It was cold, frosty weather. Two days and two nights we traveled. . . . When we gets to the Yankee camp all our troubles was over. . . . Yessum, iffen you could get to the Yankee's camp you was free right now.[32]

Some runaways, having made their break for freedom, reached the Union lines with little trouble. But others endured terrible ordeals. Among the latter was Cato Wareing, who fled a lowcountry South Carolina rice plantation in 1862, hoping to reach one of the Union-held Sea Islands. A vigorous man in his sixties, Wareing was the plantation overseer.[33] Besides supervising the work of the field hands, he was charged with administering the almost daily whippings ordered by his master. After the war began, the master—"a bad man," in Wareing's view—insisted that his overseer drive the hands harder and harder. At last Wareing felt compelled to plead for mercy. He told his master that the hands had reached their limit: no more could be demanded of them. The master became enraged, cursed Wareing, and sentenced him to be whipped the next day.[34]

Wareing immediately made up his mind to flee. But he told no one, not even his wife. He left the next morning, well before daylight, paddling a dugout canoe through the surrounding swampland, hoping thereby to elude the hounds that were sure to be put on his trail. After three days, during which he had nothing to eat, he realized that he was lost, abandoned the canoe, and took to the road. Thereafter he wandered, traveling by night and hiding by day. Sometimes he managed to steal food, sometimes he got handouts from slaves he approached surreptitiously; but mostly he went hungry. On one occasion he was spotted by a white woman, but he stayed calm and kept his wits about him. Greeting her deferentially, he made up a story on the spot to account for his presence—a story believable enough that he wound up getting a meal from her, after which he coolly resumed his journey. On another occasion he barely escaped mauling by a dog that came at him. He drove the animal off with his walking stick, but other dogs were soon after him. He had to take to the water again and ended up wading for hours. Twice during his long trek he narrowly avoided capture by Rebel army scouts. At last, after learning from a black man that a Union gunboat was anchored in a river nearby, Wareing stole a rowboat, made his way to the vessel, and was taken aboard. "[W]en I git on de [gun]boat," as he later recounted, "I thought I was in hebben." This deliverance came near the end of June 1862—more than five weeks after he left the plantation.[35]

A few of the very boldest escapees returned after a time to bring away loved ones left behind. A Floridian named Robert Sutton undertook one such daring mission. Relying on his knowledge of the St. Mary's River, where he had spent years piloting steamboats, Sutton had fled alone one night in 1862 from his home in the village of Woodstock, 40 miles up from where the river flowed into the Atlantic Ocean. Down the river he went in a dugout canoe, eventually reaching the Yankee forces on the Sea Islands. But he never forgot the wife and child he had left in Woodstock, and before much time passed he stealthily made his way back to them and spirited them away under his master's nose.[36]

Slaves in the Border states (the nonseceding Southern states of Maryland, Delaware, Kentucky, and Missouri) had an experience different in many ways from that of slaves in the invaded sections of the Confederacy. These states were occupied by Yankee forces very early in the war and heavily garrisoned throughout it, but because they remained in the Union they were generally not subjected to martial law, and state and local governmental authority persisted there. Moreover, these states (along with the new Border state of West Virginia, created in 1863 from the western counties of Virginia) were exempted from the Emancipation Proclamation, and Union troops stationed there honored that rule more often than those stationed in the exempted areas of the Confederate South. In the end, however, freedom came to the Border states, driven by the slaves' unquenchable thirst for liberty and the overwhelming momentum of war.

Enslaved people in the Border states grew restless wherever Union troops were on hand. Sometimes soldiers came to their aid. Three Maryland slaves, a young man and two teenaged boys, were among those who benefited from such assistance. After deserting their master in the fall of 1861 they took refuge in a nearby army camp. When their master, a man named Smoot, learned where they were and came to claim them, the colonel in command allowed him to search the camp but cautioned him, as Smoot later reported, that "I might meet with some difficulty as a portion of his troops were abolitionist." This warning turned out to be something of an understatement. "[As] soon as my mission become general[ly] known," wrote Smoot, "a large crowd [of soldiers] collected and followed me crying shoot him, bayonet him, kill him, pitch him out, the nigger Stealer. . . . [T]heir threats were accompanied with a few stones thrown at me which very soon became an allmost continued shower of stones a number of which struck me. . . . [T]he officer who accompanied me took no notice of what was going on." Afraid for his life, Smoot retreated from the camp "without getting my servants." Three and a half months later, when he wrote his account of the incident, his slaves were still with the Yankees.[37]

Even as the presence of the Union army destabilized slavery in the Border states, however, the persistence of state and local authority preserved it. A bloody encounter in Prince Georges County, Maryland, in September 1863 proved that the peculiar institution was still alive there. Thirty runaways, banded together and armed with a few antiquated muskets for self-defense, were making their way through the county when they encountered a squad of patrollers. Ordered to halt, the fugitives instead resisted, but their broken-down weapons would not fire. The patrollers' weapons worked quite well, however; five of the fugitives were wounded, and they and most of the others were taken into custody. The owners of some of these runaways were in hot pursuit, and they soon arrived and dragged their bondsmen back to slavery. Five whose owners did not immediately appear were lodged in jail in the nearby town of Marlboro, one of them suffering from a blast of birdshot in his face that left him blinded.[38]

Indeed, jails throughout the Border states grew crowded with would-be fugitives. There were dozens in the Baltimore city jail by the summer of 1863, most of them having been committed by a magistrate after being arrested by the police when caught going at large. Among them was a man named Frederick Robinson, who had run away from his home on the state's eastern shore a few months after the war began but had been apprehended and had been sitting in jail ever since.[39] The municipal jail of Louisville, Kentucky, was likewise put to use in thwarting freedom-seekers. In a January 1863 letter to the army provost marshal assigned to the city, the chief of police explained "the method and manner of treating runaway negroes which are found running at large in the City. The Jail has been full for several months. . . . My orders to the Police have been, to commit [runaways] according to law. . . . In every instance the owner is written to, immediately. This course has very generally been persued and many have been returned to their owners by this plan."[40]

State and local courts likewise bolstered the institution of slavery in the Border states. In November 1863 a court in Charles County, Maryland, sentenced three black men (two of them legally free, one a slave) to 11 years and 11 months in the state penitentiary for aiding the escape of slaves; they were still in the penitentiary when the war ended.[41] Some Missouri slaveowners tried to curtail the exodus of their slaves by bringing criminal charges against whites who employed runaways (under the state law regarding "Unlawfully dealing with slaves") and by suing the employers in civil court for the value of the wages paid; the civil authorities accepted such claims and proceeded with the cases.[42]

Civil officials in the Border states also preserved the system of slave sales. In 1863 the sheriff of Bullitt County, Kentucky, duly put on the auction block the runaway Margaret and her four daughters, who remained unclaimed by their owner after having been held in jail since their capture and advertised as the law required. In ordering the sale, the county court stipulated only that Margaret and her youngest child, a two-year-old, be sold together. At the auction, held on the county courthouse steps on May 18, a man named James Funk bought Margaret and her youngest for $535. The other girls—ages 6, 8, and 11—were each purchased by a different buyer.[43]

Federal authorities were often reluctant to interfere with slavery in the Border states. Louisville provides an example. The city police chief who wrote to the provost marshal in January 1863 about jailed runaways asked if the course he was pursuing was acceptable. The provost marshal replied that the military commander of that district preferred to stay out of civil affairs and advised the chief to "execute the Civil Law, as you understand it."[44]

Faced with persisting state and local authority and the reluctance of many federal officials to intervene, some freedom-seeking slaves in the Border states seized the opportunity (unavailable to slaves in the Confederacy) provided by the proximity of free territory. Numbers of Maryland and Delaware slaves made their way to Pennsylvania, and some Kentucky slaves crossed the Ohio River. (Those who took these northward-leading paths were following in the footsteps of prewar fugitives who had found sanctuary in the North, some with the aid of the so-called Underground Railroad.) After Congress abolished slavery in Washington, D.C., in April 1862, many Maryland runaways made that city their destination.[45] These included 37 Charles County slaves who deserted their master one Saturday night in June 1862. "[O]ld and young, hale and infirm, packed off bag and baggage," a local newspaper reported. "These stampedes are becoming common."[46]

Slavery in the Border states could not withstand indefinitely the challenges and pressures that accumulated as the war continued. The flagrant stampedes and quiet exoduses that whites railed against multiplied over time, while federal authorities' acquiescence in slavery's continued existence dwindled. The decision to recruit black men as Union soldiers dealt an especially heavy blow to the already staggering institution. The army began wholesale enlistment of able-bodied black men in the seceded states and the free states in early 1863; those who were slaves were deemed free upon enlistment. Recruiting was extended to Maryland and Missouri in mid-1863 and Kentucky in early 1864. Enlistment in the Border states was hedged about with restrictions at first—for example, slaves were in some cases required to have their master's permission to sign up—but the restrictions eventually fell by the wayside, allowing enlistment to proceed virtually unhindered. Moreover, the army offered cash bounties to Unionist masters who permitted their slaves to enlist, and some, sensing that their human property would soon be lost to them anyway, accepted the offer. And even before Border state slaves could enlist legally in their home states, thousands got into the army by deserting their masters and slipping across the state line to the nearest federal post in a seceded or free state—Kentucky slaves into Tennessee, for example, and Missouri slaves into Kansas.[47]

Once enlistment was under way in the Border states, federal recruiters did not always wait for enlistees to come to them. It was common for army recruitment squads to range through the countryside or prowl the rivers and coastlines in steamboats, gathering in all the black men who wanted to enlist (and some who did not, for recruiters sometimes filled the ranks by force).[48] The village of Snow Hill on Maryland's eastern shore experienced one such visitation. On a Saturday in the fall of 1863 the steamer *John Tracey* tied up at the village wharf on the Pocomoke River, having come many miles up from Chesapeake Bay. On board were a squad of black soldiers, a brass band of black musicians, and a Union army recruiting officer named William Birney. Colonel Birney announced that recruits were welcome, the band played, and word spread quickly through the community. Slaves flocked to the wharf and climbed aboard the steamer, nicknaming it "Jesus" for the salvation it brought. Birney apparently turned none away, not even women and children. When the *John Tracey* headed back down the river on Monday, 200 black people were aboard—"some owners," the local newspaper reported, "losing every one they had."[49]

Well before the war's third year ended it was obvious that slavery in the Border states was *in extremis*. The attitude of federal authorities toward the institution was growing more hostile, open defiance of masters by slaves was becoming commonplace, and the ability of state and local authorities to enforce the slave codes was waning. A Maryland newspaper editor informed his readers in September 1863 that "The slaves have been leaving our county [Montgomery] in so continuous a stream as to leave most of our farmers [without] help to save their fodder, corn, and other outstanding crops." Indeed, he warned, the farmers might well have to "abandon their pursuits altogether."[50] In another part of Maryland the following month an editor likewise reported the massive desertion of slaves and observed that "the tenure to this species of property has become so insecure as to render it entire[ly] valueless."[51] This was hardly an exaggeration. Where slave sales were still being held, demand was generally weak and buyers scarce. When the estate of a deceased slaveholder of Washington County, Maryland, was inventoried and appraised in March 1864 in preparation for distribution to heirs, the 17 slaves who were part of the estate were valued at $5 apiece.[52]

Community by community, slavery disintegrated in the Border states. "Our system of labor is utterly demoralized," a Louisville newspaper reported in late 1864. "[N]o family know when they rise in the morning whether they have a servant to prepare breakfast for them or not."[53] The diary of a rural Kentucky slaveowner chronicled the demise of slavery in his neighborhood in the first months of 1864, as enslaved men, women, and children left their homes and headed for the nearest army post. The date of the institution's death on his place could be fixed quite precisely. It was June 8: "A day of strange feelings!," he wrote. "Found my plantation entirely deserted by negroes—not one left!"[54]

For many Border state slaves, freedom came without the necessity of flight. Henry Clay Bruce of Chariton County, Missouri, told in his memoir of his master, who, with slavery crumbling around him in late 1863, acknowledged its extinction but tried to keep his farm going by enticing his black workers to stay. He "used every persuasive means possible to prevent [our leaving]. . . . He gave every grown person a free pass, and agreed to give me fifteen dollars per month, with board and clothing, if I would remain with him." Bruce accepted the offer, and on January 1, 1864, began his new life as a free, wage-earning man.[55] Some Border state masters, on the other hand, acknowledged slavery's end by driving away any black people who remained with them. Most were women and children whose husbands and fathers had previously left—in some cases, to join the Union army. "[T]hey being found rather unprofitable, and expensive [to support]," wrote a Union officer in Missouri a few months before the war's end, the women and children "are turned loose upon the people to support—Their former owners make no provision for them, save hauling them to within a convenient distance of some military post, and set[ting] them out with orders to never return home—telling them they are free."[56] In March 1865 the enslaved wives and children of Union soldiers in the Border states and everywhere else in the South were, by joint resolution of Congress, declared legally free.[57]

Confronting slavery's inexorable disintegration, three of the Border states bowed to reality and formally abolished the institution before the war ended. In Maryland, a constitutional convention assembled in 1864 and created a new state constitution that outlawed slavery; approved by popular referendum in October, it took effect on November 1. A constitutional convention in Missouri emancipated that state's slaves in January 1865. West Virginia, admitted to the Union in 1863 with a constitutional provision for gradual emancipation, enacted full emancipation by legislative decree in early 1865. Only Kentucky and Delaware stood against the tide, refusing to consider state emancipation in any form. The peculiar institution remained technically in force in those two states until the Thirteenth Amendment to the U.S. Constitution was ratified in December 1865. While many black people in Kentucky and Delaware thus remained legally enslaved for months after the war's end, and slaveowners and civil authorities tried to preserve the institution, few if any persons there were actually held as slaves against their will after the spring of 1865.[58]

Exactly how many Southern slaves became free before the Civil War ended is impossible to say; only a rough estimate can be calculated. Adding the 1860 slave population figures for the Border states, the western counties of Virginia, and the District of Columbia and deducting a portion (5%) as an estimate of the number of slaves removed by their masters to secure regions inside the Confederacy yields a figure of about 420,000. To that should be added the 1860 slave population of Tennessee (which came entirely under Union army control before the war ended), minus removed slaves (say 10%): this comes to about 250,000. One historian's reasonable estimate of the aggregate number of formerly enslaved people within Union lines in Louisiana, South Carolina, North Carolina, and the tidewater and eastern shore sections of Virginia by the spring of 1865 is 230,000. Adding an educated guess about the number of Georgia, Florida, Alabama, Mississippi, Arkansas, and Texas slaves (and slaves from the other sections of Virginia) who escaped to Union lines or otherwise gained freedom during the war yields a grand total of a little less than a million—that is, approximately one Southern slave of every four.[59]

One of the most remarkable things about wartime emancipation is the near absence of vengefulness among the freed people. Even those who had suffered at the hands of cruel masters rarely sought to get even when they had the chance. A few slaves did gain some satisfaction from informing on their owners. One was Humphrey, who lived on a middle Tennessee plantation and in 1864 revealed to a Yankee foraging squad where his mistress had hidden her horses. The soldiers seized the animals, despite the mistress's tearful pleading. "Oh how enraged I was at [Humphrey's] perfidy," she later wrote, adding that after he had directed the Yankees to the hiding place "that old devil . . . walked off himself and has not been seen since."[60] In west Tennessee in 1862, a wealthy slaveowner named Ray was confronted by a Yankee officer who had heard that he had provided shoes for the Confederate army; Ray denied the charge, but some of his slaves affirmed its truth and then watched with delight as the officer marched their master away under arrest. "Mr. Ray used to abuse his negroes," the officer reported, "and they consequently entertain no friendly feelings for him."[61] On rare occasions liberated slaves threatened or abused their master. A Union soldier named Jake, who took part in an expedition up the St. John's River in Florida in 1863, found himself at the very plantation from which he had escaped a few months earlier. He had been owned by a man named Reed, who at some point in the past had separated Jake and his wife and sold her off to Georgia. Still burning with rage, Jake now shouldered his musket, marched up to the Big House, and demanded to meet Reed "face to face" so that he could "teach him what it is to part man and wife." Informed by Reed's daughter that the planter was not there, Jake departed, leaving the woman unmolested but deeply frightened.[62] Such incidents were few, however. The vast majority of slaves sought only freedom, not vengeance. A Northern missionary who worked among the freed people in Tennessee in 1864 was deeply impressed, as he recorded in his diary, by "the general absense of a feeling of revenge or spirit of retaliation towards those who have oppressed, and in some cases brutally maltreated them."[63]

All but a handful of the freed people of the wartime South hailed their liberation joyfully and with malice toward none. Their exultation was tempered, however, by their understanding that they must now make their way in a world very different from that they had known. What shape this new world would assume was uncertain, for the precise nature of the freedom that the liberated people had gained was yet to be defined.

Rouge about that time wrote of the blacks who had come into town from outlying plantations and were now being solicited by their former owners to return to work: some were willing to take the planters up on their offer of $10 a month in wages, "but not one inch will they go except they get one month in advance."[2]

Many laborers and planters soon came to terms, through informal agreements or formal contracts. A Kentuckian named Abram, who had fled his master's farm in June 1864 and sought refuge in the distant city of Louisville, returned later "professing a settled purpose to stay at home," as his erstwhile owner reported. By January 1865 the two had worked out a share arrangement: Abram would get to keep a fourth of the tobacco crop he made.[3] Eight Arkansans—five women, two men, and a girl—signed a one-year contract with their ex-master in January 1864 by which they were guaranteed rations, clothing, and a third of the crop, agreeing in return "to work diligently and industriously to raise said crop and to behave themselves in an orderly manner."[4]

The U.S. government intervened in the labor issue and played a key role in the evolving free-labor system. In most areas of the South under martial law—particularly along the Mississippi River, in the Louisiana sugar parishes, and on the Sea Islands—army or Treasury Department officials laid down and enforced detailed rules for employing freed people. These rules varied by locality and changed over time, but in general they were meant to ensure both that slavery was not reinstated (compensation for labor was required, corporal punishment forbidden, and so forth) and that the freed people were not idle and dependent on government support. Many plantations in the occupied regions that had been abandoned by their owners were seized by the U.S. government and leased to Northern entrepreneurs, who in turn hired freed people to work them.[5]

Freed people were not, in general, encouraged by the government to establish themselves independently. But there were a couple of notable exceptions. One was at a place called Davis Bend, on the Mississippi River 30 miles south of Vicksburg, where several large plantations—one of them Jefferson Davis's—were located. When the Union army and navy took control of the area in 1863 planters and overseers fled. But some of the slaves stayed on, and as time passed they were joined by fugitives from surrounding areas. In November 1864, following an earlier suggestion by General Ulysses S. Grant, army officials designated the Bend a special enclave or colony to be worked by blacks alone. They invited those who were there (individuals and families) to form themselves into small collectives and lease plots of land. Seed, work animals, equipment, and rations, would be provided on credit by the government or civilian entrepreneurs. The Davis Bend freed people accepted the offer eagerly. By the beginning of the 1865 planting season, some 1,750 black men, women, and children had come together in 181 collectives, each with between 3 and 25 able-bodied hands. They cultivated a total of 5,000 acres, growing food for sustenance and cotton for profit. Even here, however, the freed people did not enjoy full autonomy. The army appointed three white supervisors to enforce the official regulations that governed the colony and to oversee matters generally.[6]

At that very time, hundreds of miles to the east, another experiment in black self-sufficiency was going forward at the behest of a Union general. William T. Sherman, having arrived in Savannah after leading his army on its famous "march to the sea," pondered what to do about the slaves liberated during the campaign just ended and the campaign he would soon undertake northward into the Carolinas. Thousands had followed his army to Savannah, imposing (in Sherman's view) a dangerous and unnecessary burden. In the city he met with a group of black ministers, who told him that what freed people wanted and needed most was land of their own. To gratify that desire, but more especially to rid his army of fugitive slaves, Sherman issued Special Field Orders No. 15 on January 16, 1865. This decreed that, in the region from Charleston, South Carolina, to north Florida, all the Sea Islands, all the abandoned rice plantations within 30 miles of the coast, and all the land bordering the St. Johns River in Florida were to be "reserved and set apart for the settlement of the [freed] negroes." Each black family there could claim a 40-acre plot and work it independently. A Union army officer was appointed to supervise claims and settlement. In no way did Sherman intend this program to constitute reparations to the former slaves for their years of unrequited toil; nor did he see it as a model to be followed throughout the occupied South. For him it was simply a practical, short-term solution to the specific problem of black refugees trailing his army. But to many freed people it represented a glorious vision of the future, and it would inspire, in the postwar period, a call for "forty acres and a mule" for every black family to compensate them for their years of enslavement and to ensure their economic independence. By April 1865 some 20,000 black people were living and working under the terms of this "Sherman grant."[7] The great majority, however, were very likely confined to the Sea Islands and the St. Johns River banks, where Union military forces were on hand; the coastal rice districts of South Carolina and Georgia were not under Union control until after the war ended, and until then were dangerous places for freed blacks to settle.

Beyond the boundaries of the Sherman grant and Davis Bend, the great majority of freed workers found it necessary to come to terms with white employers, either on their own or with federal oversight. Sometimes workers and employers got along agreeably and productively. Such was the case on Nimrod Porter's plantation, on the outskirts of the occupied town of Columbia in middle Tennessee. A good number of the slaves on the place stayed on contentedly as freed people, for Porter had been a benevolent master and now proved to be a decent employer. Some agreed to work for share wages, others for cash wages; one, named Caleb, rented a section of the plantation and built a cabin on it. Porter was pleased with the new arrangements: "The boys are working verry well," he wrote in his journal on March 7, 1865. A couple of weeks later he specifically commended William, who "has been issuing out the rations for the blacks & feed for the horses & is attending to that branch of business which requires a good deal of attention."[8]

No such harmony prevailed, however, on many other places where former masters and former slaves were seeking to define the terms of freedom. Even if the matter of compensation was settled, any number of other issues could cause trouble. A planter in Lafourche Parish, Louisiana, complained to the local provost marshal in February 1865 that his laborers' indolence over the past year had resulted in a "meager crop": "[T]he sun was high when they commenced to work and not set when they quitted. . . . I urged [them] very often . . . to be more diligent and not to spend every Saturday afternoon in idleness. . . . [A] stubborn refusal was all I met on every point." He asked permission to withhold part of their pay.[9] In 1864 an overseer on a Natchez-area plantation wrote of the "outrageous conduct" of his hired hands, "who will not work for love or money. . . . [T]hey go out about 10 or 11 o'clock, pick 25 or 30 lbs [of cotton] and return to their quarters, stealing fences, boards & even portions of their houses with which to make fires to warm themselves and cook the hogs and beef they may have killed during the day—and this notwithstanding they are furnished with wood and their regular rations."[10]

Complaints like this about the hired freed people were no doubt justified in some cases, but so were many of the freed people's complaints about their employers. Filching firewood and hogs could be a protest against a stingy employer's refusal to supply enough provisions to live on; taking Saturday afternoons off could represent merely a desire to adopt the same work schedule that white farmers had always enjoyed. A perceptive assessment of the labor issue came from the pen of the provost marshal of Jefferson Parish, Louisiana, who had to deal with many disputes. In June 1863 he observed that

> The planters and overseers do not sufficiently appreciate, or regard, the change that has taken place, especially in respect to this institution of slavery. The negroes come back on to the plantation, with altogether different feelings, from those of former times. They have obtained in the [Union army] camps, and wherever they have been, and they exhibit, a spirit of independance—a feeling, that they are no longer slaves, but hired laborers; and demand to be treated as such. They will not endure the same treatment, the same customs, and rules—the same language—that they have heretofore quietly submitted to.
>
> This feeling is in many cases, either entirely ignored, or not sufficiently respected, by those who have charge of them on the plantations, and the consequence is, trouble, immediately—and the negroes band together, and lay down their own rules, as to when, and how long they will work &c &c. and the Overseer loses all control over them.[11]

A few freed people, like Caleb on the Porter place, managed to stake out a measure of independence by renting a plot of land and working it without supervision. In March 1864 freedman Washington Keats made his mark on a one-year contract with plantation owner Maria Thibault of Pulaski County, Arkansas. Keats would rent a 100-acre section of the plantation for $400, "to be paid after the [cotton] crop is made, and before it is removed from said land"; he also agreed to "furnish [Thibault] vegetables and fruit for family use."[12] In March 1865 three freed men in the Vicksburg, Mississippi, area—George Walton, Cato Darden, and Ephraim Watkins—agreed to rent an 80-acre tract from widow Sarah Lane for that agricultural season. The rent was $600, $200 of which was due when the contract was signed, the balance by September 1.[13] As these contracts suggest, renting usually required a substantial outlay of cash before the crop was sold at market, and it was therefore beyond the means of the great majority of freed slaves.

Many Southern whites insisted that the considerable degree of autonomy that renting a farm represented should be altogether denied to the freed people (not to mention owning a farm, the very embodiment of yeoman autonomy). Blacks, they said, must be always a dependent, closely supervised laboring class, never an independent landed class. Many insisted furthermore that the black laborer's right to negotiate with an employer for the best terms must be narrowly circumscribed. In the districts where army or Treasury Department labor regulations were in force, white landowners and other employers found their hands tied; but elsewhere many took steps to systematically deny blacks the full enjoyment of the rights of free workers. In doing so they foreshadowed one of the most contentious issues of the postwar years.

It was in Maryland that this effort was most conspicuous. On November 9, 1864, just eight days after the state emancipation amendment took effect, a number of Prince Georges County landholders assembled for a public meeting at Marlboro, the county seat. After due deliberation they unanimously adopted a set of resolutions that they pledged to abide by and that they "earnestly recommend[ed]" to all other employers in the county. They agreed, first, not to hire any black field hands except under 12-month contracts (fearing that daily, weekly, or monthly arrangements would give workers too much flexibility and leverage) and, second, not to entice hands away from other employers by offering better terms. They furthermore agreed to a wage scale: they would pay a maximum of $120 per year and board for "First-class negro men"; $50 and board for "first-class negro women, (without children)"; $60 and board for boys under 18.[14] Six days later another such meeting convened in Port Tobacco in Charles County. The attendees passed a similar set of resolutions, but added one urging landowners not to rent a house or land to blacks "unless such house or land is kept under the control and supervision of the proprietor or owner thereof, so as to prevent such house or land from being the resort of the idle, vicious and dishonest of this class."[15] Other meetings of the same sort took place around the state.[16]

Another aspect of the Maryland employers' preemptive strike against freed peoples' labor rights was a concerted effort, with the connivance of state and local courts, to bind black youths of working age as indentured servants. Here the employers took advantage of a state law enacted before the war that permitted the apprenticing to whites of free-black children whose parents were deceased or unable to care for them. The law required no compensation for the labor beyond room and board and clothing, and (unlike a similar law regarding white orphans) imposed no requirement that the child be taught the so-called three R's (reading, writing, and arithmetic). A huge wave of these legal actions followed emancipation in the state, in almost every case instigated by the child's former owner, and against the wishes of the child and his or her parents. Whites who secured these court-approved apprenticeships gained not only the cheap, compulsory labor of the children—girls until age 18, boys until age 21—but also a useful device for keeping the children's parents tied to the old home place. An outraged provost marshal in Talbot County explained in November 1864 how the law was perverted to carry out the scheme:

> In many instances, boys of 12 and 14 years are taken from their parents, under the pretence that they (the parents) are incapable of supporting them, while the younger children are left to be maintained by the parents. This is done without obtaining the parent's consent, and in direct violation of the provisions of the Act. . . . My office is visited every day by numbers of these poor creatures, asking for redress, which I have not the power to give. They protest before the Court against binding their children to their former masters . . . and yet that same Court declares them vagrants.[17]

While most of the people liberated during the war stayed on, or soon returned to, farms or plantations and struggled for their rights there, many others experienced freedom elsewhere. The Union army camps and posts to which thousands fled provided not only a refuge but, for some, a job. The army needed all the labor it could get, and many fugitives were glad to provide it. One who found work with the Yankees was Boston Blackwell, the 15-year-old (mentioned in chapter 4) who abandoned his Arkansas plantation home in 1863 to avoid a whipping from an angry overseer; after two days and two nights of flight, he reached the occupied town of Pine Bluff, where he hired on with the Quartermaster department as a wagon driver.[18] He was one of many who took up that kind of work. The Union Army of the Cumberland alone employed by 1864 some 4,000 formerly enslaved men as teamsters; as one Union officer noted, the army preferred Southern blacks for that job because they were more familiar with mules and more attentive to their duties than "careless white drivers."[19] Other black men and boys took up pick, spade, or axe to labor on the Yankees' fortifications and railroad tracks; others hired on as officers' servants. Many women and girls found work as army laundresses, cooks, or nurses. While such labor paralleled that being done by many thousands of other black people for the Confederate army (as discussed in chapter 3), there was of course a fundamental difference: those within the Union lines were usually free to choose their job (and to quit it), and they usually got wages.[20]

As the number of black people in the Union camps and posts multiplied, army authorities had to confront the problems of housing and subsistence. Jobs could not immediately be found for all of them, and many—being very old or young, disabled, or burdened with small children—could not work anyway. Union officials therefore began, by late 1862, to set up facilities to provide for those needing help. Dubbed "contraband camps" (from the nickname "contrabands" for slaves who came into Union lines, so called because one Union general had refused to return them to their owners on the grounds that they were contraband of war), these were generally located on the outskirts of garrisoned towns. They eventually numbered nearly 100 and served as temporary homes for tens of thousands of black refugees. In middle and west Tennessee alone at least 15 contraband camps were operating at one time or another during the war. The one at Murfreesboro had 2,000 residents by early 1864; that on President's Island near Memphis had half again that number by the summer of 1864. Contraband camp residents received housing, rations, clothing, and medical care. Northern humanitarian agencies sent clothes, blankets, medicines, and other supplies to the camps to supplement the army provisions, along with civilian volunteers to distribute the supplies and help administer the camps.[21]

The contraband camps were never intended to be more than temporary shelters. Army authorities viewed them primarily as labor depots, and they encouraged—and often forced—the able-bodied residents to find employment. Those who could work or serve in uniform generally spent little time in the camps before they went off to the army, or to free-labor farms and plantations, or to the shops and households of whites needing them for nonagricultural work. Because men in the prime of life were generally more employable than others, the camps were mostly populated by children, their mothers, and the elderly. For example, of the 3,657 people in the Corinth, Mississippi, camp in March 1863, there were 1,440 women, 1,559 children, and only 658 men; and the number of men there declined further in the succeeding months as the Union army began recruiting black soldiers. Some of the men, women, and children who remained in the contraband camps performed nonremunerative chores there: cooking, laundering, nursing, chopping firewood, and tending vegetable gardens and livestock.[22]

Many freed people (probably most) who left the farms and plantations avoided the contraband camps and army camps and instead took up residence in the larger towns and cities under Union control—thus following in the footsteps of a great many free blacks of the antebellum years, who had found a measure of security and independence by moving to urban areas. Black communities sprang up and grew prolifically during the war years in Memphis, Nashville, Alexandria (Virginia), and numerous other places where there had been none before, while preexisting black communities in such places as New Orleans and Baltimore expanded enormously. The newly arrived black residents found work of all sorts, some as military or municipal laborers, others as servants, cooks, waiters, barmaids, laundresses, nurses, stevedores, draymen, or hack drivers. A few with special skills managed to set themselves up in a trade such as barbering or a profession such as the ministry. The newly founded communities were physically little more than shanty-towns, but they bustled with activity and nurtured the seeds of an urban black culture that would blossom and flourish in the postwar years.[23]

This vibrant black communalism encouraged in many of the urban freed people, newcomers and old residents alike, a particularly forceful assertiveness and an expansive vision of the future. It was in the cities that the desire for full racial equality was most loudly and articulately proclaimed.[24] Nashville's black community raised its voice in January 1865, when an all-white Unionist convention assembled in the city to rewrite Tennessee's constitution and restore its civil government. Sixty-two black men of Nashville presented a lengthy petition to the convention. It urged the delegates not only to formally abolish slavery—"one of the greatest crimes in all history"—but also to grant legal rights and the franchise to "our unfortunate and long suffering race." The petitioners reminded the convention that "This is a democracy—a government of the people. It should aim to make every man, without regard to the color of his skin, the amount of his wealth, or the character of his religious faith, feel personally interested in its welfare." Blacks were fully prepared to exercise such rights, the petitioners declared: "We know the burdens of citizenship, and are ready to bear them. We know the duties of a good citizen, and are ready to perform them cheerfully."[25]

The impulse that drew many freed people away from the homes they had long known and toward places new and sometimes far away was a kind of wanderlust, a reaction against the enforced immobility of bondage.[26] A Nashville slaveholder who testified in late 1863 before a commission investigating the condition of blacks recognized this impulse but found it puzzling. She "said she had seven slaves," the commission's scribe recorded. "They were well clothed and fed, their rooms nicely carpeted, and their beds comfortable, and she said she would be willing to pay them wages, but they were unwilling to stay, because they thought they would not be free unless they went away."[27]

Many who identified freedom with mobility marched with a musket in their hands. From the conflict's very beginning some black men burned with a desire to serve the Union cause as soldiers; but black recruitment was controversial among the Northern public and in the government, and it remained so even after the matter of emancipation had been decided by the Lincoln administration and Congress. The first blacks to don Union army uniforms did so on the South Carolina Sea Islands in the spring of 1862, when General David Hunter began—without permission from Washington—to organize an infantry regiment from among the contrabands there. Overruled by his superiors, Hunter formally disbanded the regiment in early August, but one company of it remained intact. Late that month, after another officer on the Sea Islands asked for and received War Department permission to recruit blacks, that company became the nucleus of the 1st South Carolina Infantry Regiment. It was later joined by the 2nd South Carolina, recruited in January 1863. In the meantime, a few other officers in the occupied South and civil officials in the Union states had begun organizing black regiments on their own initiative, some with official permission, some without. But as late as March 1863 there were only a handful of such units in service and President Lincoln still hesitated—from fear of a political backlash in the North and from doubt that blacks would make good soldiers—to order extensive, systematic recruitment. Near the end of March, however, having received glowing reports about some of the black units, and by then confident of the support of a majority of Congress and the Northern public, he ordered the Secretary of War to begin full-scale recruitment. The secretary complied, and soon thereafter established a Bureau for Colored Troops to oversee the raising, officering, and equipping of black units (it was understood from the start that black soldiers were to be segregated in separate units officered by whites). Recruitment was limited at first to the Confederate states and the North, but eventually extended (as noted in chapter 4) to the Border states.[28]

By war's end, some 179,000 black men were serving, or had served, in the Union army. Of these, 99,000 were from the Confederate states and 42,000 from the Border states, with the remainder from the North and West. Kentucky and Louisiana provided more than any other states (24,000 each), with Tennessee not far behind (20,000). The Kentucky total is especially impressive, for it represents nearly 6 of every 10 black men in that state ages 18 to 45. These 179,000 black soldiers served in 120 infantry regiments, 7 cavalry regiments, 12 heavy artillery regiments, and 10 light artillery companies. Another 9,600 black men served during the war in the Union navy, which had accepted blacks even before the war.[29]

A few who cast off the bonds of slavery during the war experienced freedom not on farms or plantations, nor in the army camps or contraband camps, nor in the urban communities, nor in the army or navy, but in hidden refuges independent of any authority. In this they resembled the so-called maroons of earlier times, runaway slaves who banded together in the swamps of North America or the rugged island interiors of the Caribbean and subsisted by hunting, fishing, stock-raising, gardening, and sometimes plundering. Such a colony had taken shape by late 1861 on Edisto Island, just off the South Carolina mainland. Whites had abandoned the island when Union army and navy forces arrived in the area in early November of that year, but no Union troops were actually posted on Edisto. By early 1862 there were probably a hundred or more formerly enslaved people living there, some of the men armed with muskets to protect the independence of their little community.[30] Other such communities, cloistered and vigilant, sprang up elsewhere. A young Louisiana man named Octave Johnson told of his experience hiding out in a remote section of St. James Parish, where he had fled (probably in 1861 or 1862) after his overseer threatened him with a whipping: "I ran away to the woods, where I remained for a year and a half; I had to steal my food; took turkeys, chickens and pigs; before I left [the hiding place] our number had increased to thirty, of whom ten were women; . . . sometimes we would rope beef cattle and drag them out to our hiding place . . . ; we slept on logs and burned cypress leaves to make a smoke and keep away mosquitoes." Tracked down at last by a white man with bloodhounds, Johnson and some of his companions dove into a bayou to escape and eventually made their way down the Mississippi River to a Union post near New Orleans.[31]

Freed people celebrated and exploited their freedom in many ways. Some, especially in the urban black enclaves and the contraband camps, held "jubilees" to mark some notable event or simply to exult in the feeling of freedom. The signing of the Emancipation Proclamation evoked many such celebrations. One took place at a small contraband camp located at Twelfth and Q streets in Washington, D.C. It began four hours before midnight on December 31, 1862, when 300 black people gathered in and around the camp's schoolhouse. There an official of the Quartermaster department entertained them with a song in honor of the Proclamation, following which the camp superintendent gave a speech about the war and emancipation, adding some advice on how the freed people should conduct themselves. These preliminaries out of the way, the celebrants took control of the ceremony. A reporter for the Washington *Star* described what followed:

> Several of the negroes then [spoke], occupying the time until about two minutes before 12 o'clock, when the superintendent requested [all in the crowd] to kneel, and at once the whole number dropped on their knees in silent prayer. About two minutes past 12, an old colored man was called on to lead in prayer, and he eloquently implored that the army might be successful, that the rebellion be speedily crushed, that the blessings of Heaven would rest on President Lincoln, and that their friends left behind in Dixie might be saved. The whole number then united in singing a Hallelujah hymn.
>
> Then came a general hand-shaking, and old and young seemed frantic with joy, singing, dancing and shouting.
>
> About one o'clock a procession was formed, and they marched around the camp singing an extemporaneous song, "I'm a Free Man," and then various hymns. The most of them afterwards returned to their quarters, but numbers were engaged in singing, &c., till daybreak.[32]

That a schoolhouse figured prominently in this jubilee was fitting, for education was one of the primary means by which freed people sought to make the most of freedom. Not all had the opportunity to gain literacy; but many did, and in great numbers young and old alike seized that opportunity.

Their teachers were mostly Northern missionaries or army chaplains. Various Yankee benevolent agencies and churches sponsored wartime teaching missions in the South to educate the freed people. The teachers they employed brought with them copies of McGuffey's *Eclectic Reader* and the other pedagogical instruments that had educated a generation of America's white youth, and they set up schools wherever freed people congregated, particularly the contraband camps and the larger free-labor plantations. There were at least 84 such schools operating in 15 occupied Louisiana parishes by November 1864, staffed by 142 teachers and enrolling nearly 9,000 students. The missionary teachers, and the army chaplains who set up schools in the camps of the black regiments, were idealistic, reformist evangelicals, earnest in their labors and sympathetic to the freed slaves. But they also tended to be patronizing and didactic. What their students needed, they believed, along with the three R's, was a stiff dose of Yankee Protestantism and middle-class moralism.[33]

Some who taught the freed people were, on the other hand, fellow black Southerners who had learned to read and write before the war. One was William Jordan, a prewar free black and preacher who started a school in a church building in Columbia, Tennessee, after the Union army captured the town in 1862. He felt called to do so, according to a local man who knew of his work, for he was convinced that "if he could teach the children to read the Bible so that they might learn of heaven, he was doing a good work."[34] In the occupied town of Knoxville, Tennessee, another prewar free black and preacher likewise began a school. Alfred Anderson was his name, and he had, as he admitted in a letter to a Northern benevolent society, only "a smaul education," being able to "Read Rite And A littel mour," but he was determined to help uplift the people of his "down troden race."[35] A teenager named Susie King became a teacher for the men of the 1st South Carolina Infantry, in which her husband served. She had learned to read and write on the sly as a slave in Savannah, thanks to some friendly whites and free blacks. After escaping to a Union gunboat in 1862 she was taken to the South Carolina island where the regiment was posted, and there she married Private Ned King of Company E. Thereafter she followed the regiment wherever it went, serving as both teacher and laundress, giving reading and writing lessons when not busy with her washtub and scrub board. "I was very happy to know my [teaching] efforts were successful in camp," she wrote in her memoir, "and also felt grateful for the appreciation of my services. I gave my services willingly for four years and three months without receiving a dollar."[36]

The appreciativeness and thirst for learning that Susie King witnessed were evident everywhere schools were conducted for the freed people. "Seems like you North folks would like to have us have some knowledge," a grateful North Carolina freed woman told a missionary in a contraband camp in New Bern. "The North Carolina folks have kept us in the dark, but you folks want to put some light into us."[37] An army chaplain in Port Hudson, Louisiana, told of the black soldiers for whom schools had been set up there: "I am sure that I never witnessed greater eagerness for study. . . . A majority of the men seem to regard their books as an indispensable portion of their equipments, and the cartridge box and spelling book are attached to the same belt. There are nearly five hundred men . . . who have learned to read quite well, and also quite a large number who are able to write. A short time ago scarcely one of these men knew a letter of the alphabet."[38] From the lips of a North Carolina child came a succinct and cogent assertion of the importance of education: asked by a missionary why black children came to school, the young one replied, "If we are *educated,* they can't make slaves of us again."[39]

Another way freed people exploited and enriched their freedom was by reuniting severed families. The sacred bonds of kinship that had been forged under slavery but then broken by a master's whim or by the circumstances of war were, in some cases, restored once the infernal bonds of slavery were shattered.[40] The desperate longing and fierce determination to reunite with loved ones were exemplified by a literate freed slave from Missouri named Spotswood Rice, a private in the 67th U.S. Colored Infantry. On September 3, 1864, from an army hospital in St. Louis where he was being treated for chronic rheumatism, he wrote a letter to his daughters, Corra and Mary, who were still held in bondage back in his home town of Glasgow:

> I take my pen in hand to rite you A few lines to let you know that I have not forgot you and that I want to see you as bad as ever[.] now my Dear Children . . . be assured that I will have you if it cost me my life[.] on the 28th of the mounth 8 hundred White and 8 hundred blacke solders expects to start up the [Missouri] rivore to Glasgow . . . to be jeneraled by a jeneral that will give me both of you[.] when they Come I expect to be with them and expect to get you both. . . . If Diggs dont give you up this Government will [make him do so] . . . Oh! My Dear children how I do want to see you.[41]

The wartime reunions of black kinfolk did indeed sometimes require the use or threat of force. In Lafourche Parish, Louisiana, in February 1865—months after the Unionist state government had abolished slavery—a Union army post commander had to intervene to restore a child to her parents. The planter who held the little girl had refused to give her up, even when her father appeared at the plantation to demand her. Only after the child's mother appealed to the post commander, who then sent the planter a peremptory order, was the child released.[42]

The liberated people of the wartime South gave thanks for their liberty and the blessings it bestowed. For some, however, liberty was short-lived. Owing to the vagaries of war and the Confederate army's mandate to help preserve slavery (discussed in chapter 1), freedom gained was not always freedom maintained.

On a number of occasions a military reversal resulted in the reenslavement of contrabands. When Confederate forces recaptured the Union-occupied towns of Harpers Ferry, Virginia, in 1862; Pine Bluff, Arkansas, in 1863; Pulaski, Tennessee, in 1864; and Plymouth, North Carolina, in 1862 and again in 1864, they gathered up runaway slaves by the hundreds and marched them off to bondage. For some liberated people, the period of freedom was measured in mere hours. In Virginia in the spring of 1864, for example, Confederate troops pursuing Union cavalry raiders captured a number of blacks who were following the raiding party back to federal lines; thus did Thornton, owned by Christian Toliver of Hanover County; Joe, the slave of Thomas Harris of Louisa County; Robert, a little boy belonging to Strother Wallace of Culpeper Court House; and all the others find themselves locked up in a Richmond prison in June, awaiting the appearance of their masters to claim them. None had had more than 24 hours of freedom.[43]

In some cases the reenslavement of freed people was not merely an incident of combat but the objective of the mission. The little autonomous colony on Edisto Island, South Carolina, was targeted by a Confederate expeditionary force in January 1862.

Having learned of the presence of armed, masterless blacks on the island, General Nathan Evans ordered Colonel P. F. Stevens to deal with them. Stevens led a detachment of 120 infantrymen and 65 cavalrymen by ferry from the mainland to the island, which the troops then proceeded to sweep, ultimately rounding up 80 black men, women, and children. In the process, Stevens reported, "3 negroes were either shot or drowned and a fourth wounded; 2 women and 1 man ran into the water, and, refusing or failing to come out, were fired upon and disappeared beneath the water."[44] All the captives were taken back to the mainland; one named Billy who had borne arms was tried, convicted, and hanged. Many of the free-labor plantations along the Mississippi River were likewise targeted by Rebel troops or guerrillas, and the people working on them were carried off and reenslaved. In fact, the Confederate Secretary of War specifically ordered that this be done. In the Natchez district alone, an estimated 1,000 plantation hands were abducted by Rebel raiders in 1864.[45]

The vast majority of freed people in the wartime South remained safe from reenslavement, but the freedom they experienced was not always joyful and rewarding. Many endured hardships, abuse, or injustice. While few pined for the world of slavery they had left behind, a good many concluded that the new world of freedom was not all they had prayed for.

The cities to which many flocked became, for some, not havens of hope and opportunity but sloughs of despondency and suffering. Nashville was a particularly grim example. As the winter of 1863–64 approached, two missionaries reported on conditions there. The freed people, they wrote, "occupy old & decayed buildings, cellars & out-houses [i.e., outbuildings] as dwellings & from the insuficiency of shelter & the scarcity & high price of fuel, suffering must ensue."[46] A few weeks later a municipal official wrote a similarly depressing report: "[T]he city is overrun with negroes. . . . They crowd together in large numbers in small rooms[,] frequently from twelve to twenty living in a room not more than twenty feet square." Hygiene and health in these places were abysmal, he said; smallpox had broken out and was spreading.[47]

Squalor, crowding, and disease were not the only miseries afflicting the freed people of Nashville and other urban communities. There were too few jobs for all. Many begged for a living, and some who found jobs put themselves, as the Nashville missionaries noted, "in competition with the white population . . . for labor, thus inducing enmities & often actual collisions."[48] Some who could find no legitimate employment turned to prostitution or theft.[49]

Many of the contraband camps were not much better places to live. The camps were a low priority for the army, and some of the officials in charge were negligent. The sustenance provided was in some cases scandalously insufficient, even when supplemented by the charity of Northern benevolent associations.[50] In a March 1865 petition addressed to President Lincoln, a group of contrabands complained about the scanty rations issued (every 10 days) to the inhabitants of the camp on Roanoke Island, North Carolina: "[B]efor the Ten days is out they are going from one to another Trying to borrow a little meal to last until ration day."[51] Hulda Williams, a child during the war, recalled in old age what it was like in the Pine Bluff, Arkansas, camp: "The soldiers give each family one piece of wood every day for the camp fire, and just enough food stuff to keep the Negroes from starving. I remember my mammy would slip out at night and steal wood and scraps from the soldiers kitchen."[52] Some of the rations doled out in the camps were inedible, even nauseating. A man named Nat Black who had lived in the Nashville camp recalled being issued beef "so old . . . that when thrown against a wall it would splatter like mud."[53]

Housing and clothing, too, were often inadequate in the contraband camps. In some places nothing but tents were provided for shelter, and where barracks or cabins were built they were sometimes drafty, leaky, and overcrowded. Nat Black lived in a dirt-floor tent and suffered in the winter for lack of proper clothing. Another of his vivid memories of the Nashville camp was the lice that plagued everybody.[54] Not surprisingly, many of the contraband camps, like many of the black urban enclaves, were swept by lethal diseases. One federal official, noting the terrible death toll at a Louisiana camp in the summer of 1863, described the place as "a vast charnel house."[55] The winter of 1862–63 was a deadly time in Memphis, where as many as 1,200 blacks died in the contraband camp and urban community, and in Nashville, where the toll may have reached 1,400.[56]

Many of the blacks who worked for the army also endured harsh conditions. While Union soldiers were well clad and well fed, some contraband laborers went about ragged, shoeless, and hungry. Moreover, some were put to work against their will and not allowed to quit, some were moved unwillingly from place to place at the army's whim, some were forcibly separated from their families, and some were not paid. Some suffered all these abuses; except that they could not be bought, sold, or whipped, they could see little difference between military labor and slavery.[57]

Historical records abound with evidence of the mistreatment of black military workers. The Roanoke Islanders who petitioned the President reported that boys as young as 12 were among those taken from the contraband camp and sent more than 100 miles away to New Bern to work on fortifications, thus not only tearing them away from their mothers but also pulling them out of school. The laborers taken to New Bern from the island, men and boys alike, were supposed to get wages of $10 a month; but, as the petitioners (who were part of that workforce) explained, "we Seldom ever get the mony."[58] In some cases the procurement of black labor was nothing more than kidnapping. In Lexington, Kentucky, squads of soldiers lay in wait one Sunday outside the town's three black churches. When services ended, as one townsperson recorded in her diary, the soldiers "rushed upon the unsuspecting negroes capturing all the men they could lay hands on. The darkies in great terror ran in all directions. . . . The soldiers however caught a good many whom they sent off to Camp Nelson to work on the wagon road."[59] In April 1864 the Nashville provost guard "made a descent upon all the vagrant negroes they could find around town," a local newspaper reported. "Those furnish-ing undoubted evidence of industry and honesty were turned loose, and those fail-ing to produce such testimonials were consigned to the contraband camp, there to remain until suitable employment can be obtained for them." The ones marched off to the camp numbered about 2,000.[60] Some of them may have been among the blacks dragooned by the army to work on the Nashville & Chattanooga Railroad. These un-fortunates, as an outraged observer reported in November 1864, were turned over to contractors whose "only thought is to clutch and sease upon green Backs reguardless of the rights of the poor Negro." The contractors withheld rations from the laborers for days at a time, cheated them when measuring the wood they were paid by the cord to cut, and denied them medical care. "[T]hey dye by dozens from shere neglect."[61]

Many freed people were abused by Union soldiers who were acting in no official ca-pacity but simply out of malice. Contempt—indeed, venomous hatred—for blacks was widespread among federal troops. A soldier in middle Tennessee in 1864 admitted that "Down here the darkies . . . are really the only friends we have yet whenever they come to camp the boys curse them and threaten them."[62] A planter in north Georgia was shocked by the vicious racism of some of Sherman's troops. One of their victims, he noted in his diary, was a woman named Mamie, from whom they stole clothing, a nee-dle, and thread. "[S]he asked them to have mercy on a poor negro, they cursed her and said if she did not close her mouth they would kill her."[63] Troops posted in the middle Tennessee town of Gallatin in 1864—these not Yankees, but east Tennessee Union-ists—were described by one resident as "the meanest men I ever saw," with a particular spite against blacks. Soon after arriving they burned down a building used as a school for freed people, vowing that "they will have none of that while they stay here." That night they threatened to torch another building used by contrabands, "but the citizens told them if they did Gallatin would burn; they let it alone but say if they get up a school in it they will burn it and G[allatin] may go to H___." The post commander eventually put a stop to the east Tennesseans' mayhem, but they were heard muttering that "if Capt Nicklen leave[s] they will kill every negro in G[allatin] in less than a week."[64]

Bodily assaults on blacks by soldiers were not infrequent, and women were not ex-empt. Some Connecticut soldiers in Virginia amused themselves by seizing two black women and "turn[ing] them upon their heads, & put[ting] tobacco, chips, stocks, lighted cigars & sand into their behinds."[65] Rape and attempted rape by Union troops in the South, very rare with regard to white women, were not so with regard to black women. Some Yankees viewed enslaved women as natural prey, just as some Southern white men always had. A farmer in northern Virginia complained to a Union general in November 1861 about the troops who had repeatedly pillaged his farm, "some drunk, . . . [and] behaving in an outrageous manner. . . . [A] number of them . . . broke open my hen house & robbed it and attempted to commit a *Rape* on a servant woman."[66] Another outraged white man in that same region reported—in this case, directly to President

Lincoln—what happened on his place in April 1862, when a squad of Yankee plunderers paid a visit. One of them spotted a young slave woman and approached her, whereupon "she ran,—but he caught her and forced [her] to a Brutal act, in full view of my dwelling and Wife and two of her nieces and under the immediate eye of another soldier . . . [and within view of] seven or Eight more soldiers."[67] Even black children were victimized. One soldier in South Carolina confessed to witnessing the rape of a nine-year-old by several of his comrades.[68]

Black men who served in the Union army suffered injustices, too. For one thing, they could not rise above the rank of sergeant (though there were a handful of exceptions); and until mid-1864, when pay was equalized, they were paid barely half what white soldiers were paid. The medical care they received was generally inferior to that of white troops, and they fell victim to disease at a significantly higher rate. Furthermore, many Union commanders had no faith in black troops as combat soldiers and thus relegated them to rear-guard and fatigue duty; many spent the war with a shovel in their hands far more often than a musket.[69]

While black soldiers chafed at the inequities imposed on them, they shared the hardships that all other Civil War soldiers had to endure. Between the grating inequities and the shared hardships, there was much cause for discontent. Black soldiers did their share of grumbling, and on occasion they protested loudly. And yet most (at least most who volunteered—some, as noted in chapter 4, were forced into the ranks) never regretted their military service. That service was, for many, not only a personal path to freedom but also a willing contribution to the emancipation of all their people and a proud assertion of black equality.[70]

A soldier named Elijah Marrs exemplified the mix of impulses, personal and idealistic and patriotic, that impelled many black men to serve. A Kentuckian, he was 24 years old in September 1864, when he ran away from his master in Shelby County, made his way to Louisville with 27 other male fugitives, and enlisted in Company L of the 12th U.S. Colored Heavy Artillery. Before they fled, the fugitives had debated the idea of enlisting. Doing so would guarantee them freedom, but would of course put their lives at risk. They concluded, as Marrs wrote in his memoir, "that if we joined the army and were slain in battle, we would at least die in fighting for principle and freedom."[71]

Within hours after Marrs and his friends signed up at the Louisville provost marshal's office their owners showed up in town hunting for them, but their enlistment protected them from reenslavement. They then donned blue uniforms and set about learning the duties of a soldier. But as the stifling routine, the rigid regimentation, the threat of injury and death, and all the other burdens of army service began to weigh on him, Marrs had second thoughts about his decision to enlist. On the verge of utter discouragement, he had a talk with himself: "'[P]shaw!' said I, 'this is better than slavery, though I do march in line to the tap of the drum.' I felt freedom in my bones." He reminded himself, too, of what was at stake in the war beyond his personal freedom:

"I saw the American eagle, with outspread wings, upon the [regimental] flag, with the motto, '*E Pluribus Unum.*' . . . Then all fear [v]anished. I had quit thinking as a child and had commenced to think as a man." Religious faith also helped him persevere, as it did many of his comrades: "[A] thought seemed to come to the mind of every Christian, that though the Civil War between the North and South had separated us from home and friends, yet the protecting hand of the United Government of God was still over us all." But then came an incident in which he was irritatingly bossed around by an officer, once again stirring up resentment and doubt: "[S]till must I move at the command of a white man, and I said to myself is my condition any better now than before I entered the army?" Again, however, he reasoned with himself: "I was a soldier fighting for my freedom, and this thought filled my heart with joy. I thought, too, that the time will come when no man can say to me come and go, and I be forced to obey."[72]

Black troops fought in many Civil War engagements, exhibiting discipline and bravery that thoroughly belied the doubts about them. These combat soldiers, along with the black troops who never fired a shot in anger but did essential duty behind the lines, contributed enormously to Union victory in the war. Tens of thousands gave their lives for the cause.[73] One was Corporal William Guy of Maryland, who fell in the summer of 1864 near Petersburg, Virginia, probably on July 30 at the battle of the Crater. "I am sarry to have to inform You that thear is no do[u]bt of his Death," one of his comrades wrote to Guy's mother on August 19. "[H]e Died A Brave Death in Trying to Save the Colors of [the regiment] in that Dreadful Battil[.] Billys Death was . . . [mourned] by all." Billy, he added, had spoken often about how he looked forward to returning home after the war to his mother, wife, sister, and other loved ones. "But Providence has will[ed] other wise and You must Bow to His will."[74]

The will of Providence was on the minds of many black men and women as the war ended in the spring of 1865. The Confederacy's collapse made it certain that slavery was doomed; beyond that, however, little could be presumed. The experience of those already delivered from bondage suggested that freedom might take any number of different forms and that it would be a bitterly contested issue. What outcome Providence would impose, or allow to come about, remained to be seen.

EPILOGUE

The Confederate armies surrendered one by one in the spring of 1865, beginning with Lee's in Virginia on April 9. The Union armies, having thus accomplished their primary mission, then began in earnest the territorial conquest of Rebeldom, gradually seizing all the regions yet untouched by federal authority and the Emancipation Proclamation's mandate. As Yankee troops marched in and occupied town after town in the Confederate interior, their commanders issued edicts demanding that the Rebel citizens end all resistance to the U.S. government and release all black people from bondage. The process was slow, however—excruciatingly slow to those who awaited liberation. In some of the more remote areas of the South, especially in Texas, it was well into summer before federal power could make itself felt.[1]

Town by town, farm by farm, plantation by plantation, freedom came to those still enslaved. Typically it came after a period of uncertainty, days or weeks in which rumors abounded and blacks and whites alike tried to sort out exactly what was happening. Rarely did the Yankees have to intervene directly between master and slave as they penetrated the South in those spring and summer weeks. Rather, once it was understood that the Confederate cause was truly lost and that Union troops were in the vicinity or on the way, whites generally abandoned their commitment to preserving slavery, and masters summoned their black people to tell them they were free.[2]

Those who experienced such a moment remembered it vividly all their lives. Andrew Goodman, who had managed his master's plantation in Smith County, Texas, during the war, told an interviewer in the 1930s about his emancipation. As soon as "Marse Bob" Goodman returned home after four years in the Rebel army

> he sent for all the slaves. He was sittin' in a yard chair, all tuckered out, and sh[oo]k hands all round, and said he's glad to see us. Then he said, 'I got something to tell you. You is jus' as free as I is. You don't [be]long to nobody but you'selves. We went to the war and fought, but the Yankees done whup us, and they say the niggers is free. You can go where you wants to go, or you can stay here, jus' as you likes.' He couldn't help but cry.[3]

Three of the black families on the Goodman place soon left; the rest stayed on as hired hands. Elsewhere across the South, the newly liberated likewise made choices they had never before had the power to make. It was a time of movement and uncertainty and even bewilderment among black folk. But amid all of that, certain patterns emerged, patterns already evident in the regions where emancipation had come during the war. It became clear, for one thing, that the freed people were determined to secure sovereignty over their family relationships—sovereignty denied them as slaves—and to reunite separated families where they could. They were determined, moreover, to get just compensation for their labor. If they could labor free of white supervision, so much the better. If they could live and labor and worship in communities separate from those of whites, better still. Many freed people, moreover, particularly those who had served in uniform, were determined to seek full citizenship and equality in postwar America, with the understanding that achieving these goals would require not only legal and political rights but also economic independence and education.

There were other things revealed in the experience of the last four years and underscored in the immediate postwar months. One was the fierce determination of Southern whites to keep black people subjugated and the vast array of devices with which they could enforce such subjugation if left free to do so. Once the Confederacy collapsed, whites pledged—grudgingly—to accept black freedom, but they construed it in the narrowest way. For most it meant only that black people could no longer be bought and sold; in all other respects they must remain hewers of wood and drawers of water, condemned now and forever to inferiority and servitude. And whites were ready to use any means necessary, including violence if they could get away with it, to see that their definition of black freedom prevailed in the postwar world.

Another thing made manifest during the war and immediately after was that the U.S. government and the Northern people possessed enormous power to impose their will on the South but were, at best, uncertain allies of Southern blacks. Emancipation would never have come about without Yankee intervention, and the freed people were profoundly grateful for that intervention. However, there was plenty of evidence that many U.S. government officials and many members of the Northern public were indifferent or hostile to the freed people and would be content to bring the South back into the Union with something less than a thoroughgoing transformation of race relations.

Southern blacks' fears in this regard were intensified when news came, just days after Lee's surrender, that President Lincoln had been assassinated and that Andrew Johnson, a Southerner, would henceforth lead the nation. Sergeant Marrs of the 12th Colored Heavy Artillery told in his memoir how he and his comrades reacted:

> The morning the news reached us I had ten men and was patrolling the suburbs of [Bowling Green, Kentucky]. I marched my men out on the plain and sat down and wept. We remained there until nightfall, and then returned to town and joined with the men in camp in sorrowing over our loss. Our Moses had been slain, and we knew not what the future had in store for us. I had recourse to prayer. I threw myself on the strong arm of God, and felt that He would bring me through.[4]

It was clear to many black Southerners that the expansive freedom and autonomy they sought would be enormously difficult to achieve. But the experience of the last four years had shown that victory was possible even against great odds. The actions of Southern black people, and the yearnings and determination behind those actions, had contributed essentially to slavery's destruction; this they understood. So, too, might black aspirations and boldness prevail over enmity and inertia in the postwar world. As peace and emancipation spread through the South in the spring and summer of 1865, four million black people faced the future warily, but hopefully.

NOTES

PREFACE

1. George P. Rawick, ed., *The American Slave: A Composite Autobiography* (41 vols., Westport, CT: Greenwood Press, 1972–79), Orig. Series, 4(Pt. 2): 131.

INTRODUCTION

1. Population figures are derived from University of Virginia Library Historical Census Browser, http://fisher.lib.virginia.edu/collections/stats/histcensus (accessed June 5, 2008).

2. Rawick, *American Slave,* Suppl. Series Two, 7(Pt. 6): 2552–53.

3. Rawick, *American Slave,* Orig. Series, 14(Pt. 1): 249, Suppl. Series Two, 2(Pt. 1): 251–52, 5(Pt. 4): 1841; William Wyndham Malet, *An Errand to the South in the Summer of 1862* (London: Richard Bentley, 1863), 46.

4. Allen Parker, *Recollections of Slavery Times* (Worchester: Charles W. Burbank, 1895), 78–79, 85–86; Leon F. Litwack, *Been in the Storm So Long: The Aftermath of Slavery* (New York: Alfred A. Knopf, 1979), 23.

5. William H. Robinson, *From Log Cabin to the Pulpit; or, Fifteen Years in Slavery* (Eau Claire, WI: James H. Tifft, 1913), 76–77, 92–96; Rawick, *American Slave,* Suppl. Series Two, 6(Pt. 5): 2213–14.

6. Thomas L. Johnson, *Africa for Christ: Twenty-Eight Years a Slave* (London: Alexander and Shepheard, 1892), 24–25.

7. Henry Clay Bruce, *The New Man: Twenty-Nine Years a Slave, Twenty-Nine Years a Free Man* (York: PA: Anstadt & Sons, 1895), 99.

8. Edward Pierce, "The Contrabands at Fortress Monroe," *Atlantic Monthly* 8(1861): 638; Rawick, *American Slave,* Suppl. Series One, 3(Pt. 1): 317.

9. Robinson, *From Log Cabin to the Pulpit,* 96.

10. Malet, *Errand to the South,* 46.

11. Rawick, *American Slave,* Orig. Series, 13(Pt. 4): 192.

12. Jacob Stroyer, *My Life in the South* (Salem, MA: Salem Observer Book and Job Print, 1885), 37.

13. Johnson, *Africa for Christ,* 25.

14. Bruce, *New Man,* 99; Rawick, *American Slave,* Orig. Series, 4(Pt. 1): 11.

15. Rawick, *American Slave,* Orig. Series, 12(Pt. 1): 258.

16. Stroyer, *My Life in the South,* 38–39.

17. Mary to unnamed correspondent, n.d., *Elliott and Gonzales Family Papers,* Southern Homefront 1861–1865 Collection, Documenting the American South Digital Library, University of North Carolina, Chapel Hill, http://www.docsouth.unc.edu (accessed December 6, 2007).

CHAPTER 1

1. Arney Robinson Childs, ed., *The Private Journal of Henry William Ravenel, 1859–1887* (Columbia: University of South Carolina Press, 1947), 68.

2. Jerry Bryan Lincecum, Edward Hake Phillips, and Peggy A. Redshaw, eds., *Gideon Lincecum's Sword: Civil War Letters from the Texas Homefront* (Denton: University of North Texas Press, 2001), 280.

3. Daniel W. Crofts, ed., *Cobb's Ordeal: The Diaries of a Virginia Farmer, 1842–1872* (Athens: University of Georgia Press, 1997), 233–35.

4. Dallas *Herald,* January 9, 1861.

5. Columbus (Georgia) *Daily Columbus Enquirer,* May 14, 1861, quoting Atlanta *Intelligencer.*

6. Rawick, *American Slave,* Orig. Series, 13(Pt. 4): 192.

7. William Howard Russell, *My Diary North and South* (Boston: T.O.H.P. Burnham, 1863), 233.

8. Columbus *Daily Columbus Enquirer,* June 15, 1861, quoting Augusta *Chronicle.*

9. Savannah *Daily Morning News,* June 11, 1861.

10. Russell, *My Diary,* 132; Armstead L. Robinson, "In the Shadow of Old John Brown: Insurrection Anxiety and Confederate Mobilization, 1861–1863," *Journal of Negro History* 65(1980): 279–97.

11. Mobile *Evening News,* November 2, 1864.

12. Ira Berlin, et al., eds., *The Destruction of Slavery* (Cambridge: Cambridge University Press, 1985), 781–82.

13. Baltimore *Sun,* January 31, March 11, May 11, 1861, October 28, 1863; New Orleans *Daily True Delta,* May 28, June 7, 20, 27, 1861; E. Grey Dimond and Herman Hattaway, eds.,

Letters from Forest Place: A Plantation Family's Correspondence, 1846–1881 (Jackson: University Press of Mississippi, 1993), 233; John K. Bettersworth, *Confederate Mississippi: The People and Policies of a Cotton State in Wartime* (Baton Rouge: Louisiana State University Press, 1943), 161–63; David Williams, *Rich Man's War: Class, Caste, and Confederate Defeat in the Lower Chattahoochee Valley* (Athens: University of Georgia Press, 1998), 158; Jackson (Mississippi) *Daily Southern Crisis,* January 15, 1863.

14. New Orleans *Daily True Delta,* May 28, 1861.

15. Baltimore *Sun,* January 31, 1861.

16. Williams, *Rich Man's War,* 158.

17. Kenneth Coleman, *Confederate Athens* (Athens: University of Georgia Press, 1967), 21; Clarence L. Mohr, *On the Threshold of Freedom: Masters and Slaves in Civil War Georgia* (Athens: University of Georgia Press, 1986), 43–45; Columbus *Daily Columbus Enquirer,* January 24, 1862.

18. Baltimore *Sun,* March 14, 1861.

19. Sally E. Hadden, *Slave Patrols: Law and Violence in Virginia and the Carolinas* (Cambridge: Harvard University Press, 2001), 172–75.

20. Crofts, *Cobb's Ordeal,* 192.

21. Hadden, *Slave Patrols,* 173–74.

22. Stephen V. Ash, *When the Yankees Came: Conflict and Chaos in the Occupied South, 1861–1865* (Chapel Hill: University of North Carolina Press, 1995), 16, 237–38.

23. Ibid., 24–27.

24. John A. Dix to Abraham Lincoln, November 15, 1861, enclosing proclamation of November 13, 1861, in *The War of the Rebellion: A Compilation of the Official Records of the Union and Confederate Armies* (70 vols. in 128, Washington, D.C.: Government Printing Office, 1880–1901), Series Two, 2: 139–40.

25. *Senate Reports,* 37 Cong., 3 Sess., No. 108, Vol. 4, Serial 1154, p. 391.

26. Stephen V. Ash, *Middle Tennessee Society Transformed, 1860–1870: War and Peace in the Upper South* (Baton Rouge: Louisiana State University Press, 1988), 107; Fayetteville (Tennessee) *Union Herald,* June 18, 1862.

27. *Senate Reports,* 37 Cong., 3 Sess., No. 108, Vol. 4, Serial 1154, pp. 394–95.

28. Ash, *When the Yankees Came,* 239–41.

29. Dimond and Hattaway, *Letters from Forest Place,* 302; Parker, *Recollections of Slavery Times,* 85–86; Philip N. Racine, ed., *Piedmont Farmer: The Journals of David Golightly Harris, 1855–1870* (Knoxville: University of Tennessee Press, 1990), 314.

30. Arch Fredric Blakey, Ann Smith Lainhart, and Winston Bryant Stephens, Jr., eds., *Rose Cottage Chronicles: Civil War Letters of the Bryant-Stephens Families of North Florida* (Gainesville: University Press of Florida, 1998), 90; Rawick, *American Slave,* Orig. Series, 14(Pt. 1): 136; Pierce, "Contrabands at Fortress Monroe," 637.

31. Sarah Lois Wadley Diary, October 5, 1863, Southern Homefront 1861–1865 Collection, Documenting the American South Digital Library, University of North Carolina, Chapel Hill, http://www.docsouth.unc.edu (accessed December 11, 2007).

32. Mary to unnamed correspondent, June 8, 1862, Elliott and Gonzales Family Papers; Blakey, Lainhart, and Stephens, *Rose Cottage Chronicles,* 215.

33. Houston *Tri-Weekly Telegraph,* October 31, 1862.

34. Betsy Fleet and John D. P. Fuller, eds., *Green Mount: A Virginia Plantation Family During the Civil War* (Lexington: University of Kentucky Press, 1962), 239, 242, 244–45, 260.

35. *An Act to Provide more Efficient Police Regulations for the Districts on the Sea-board* (no publication information; probably Columbia, 1861), Confederate Imprints, 1897–1905.

36. Jackson *Weekly Mississippian,* December 3, 1862.

37. *An Ordinance Organizing and Establishing Patrols for the Police of Slaves in the Parish of St. Landry* (Opelousas: no publisher, 1863), Confederate Imprints, 1652.

38. West Baton Rouge Parish Police Jury Minutes, June 21, 1862, Special Collections, Louisiana State University.

39. St. Charles Parish Police Jury Minutes, May 19, 1862, Special Collections, Louisiana State University.

40. Mohr, *On the Threshold of Freedom,* 214–17; Hadden, *Slave Patrols,* 179–83; Fleet and Fuller, *Green Mount,* 138.

41. J. C. Pemberton to W. P. Emanuel, June 4, 1862, in *War of the Rebellion,* Series One, 14: 541.

42. J. D. Bradford to Lieutenant Colonel Sevier, January 17, 1864, in *War of the Rebellion,* Series One, 32(Pt. 2): 568.

43. Joseph Finegan to Thomas Jordan, March 20, 1863, in *War of the Rebellion,* Series One, 14: 838.

44. William Elliott to William, August 25, 1862, Elliott and Gonzales Family Papers.

45. Isaac Erwin Diary, May 27–June 6, 1863, Special Collections, Louisiana State University.

46. Stephen V. Ash, "A Wall Around Slavery: Safeguarding the Peculiar Institution on the Confederate Periphery, 1861–1865," in *Nineteenth-Century America: Essays in Honor of Paul H. Bergeron,* ed. W. Todd Groce and Stephen V. Ash (Knoxville: University of Tennessee Press, 2005), 64.

47. J. H. Wilson to John B. Chesson, no date (probably 1862), John B. Chesson Papers, North Carolina State Archives.

48. Berlin et al., *Destruction of Slavery,* 300.

49. Columbus *Daily Columbus Enquirer,* October 20, 21, 1863; Savannah *Daily Morning News,* October 19, 1863; Samuel Andrew Agnew Diary, May 12, 13, 1863, Southern Historical Collection, University of North Carolina, Chapel Hill.

50. David W. Blight, *A Slave No More: Two Men Who Escaped to Freedom, Including Their Own Narratives of Emancipation* (Orlando: Harcourt, 2007), 55–74, 219–23.

51. H. Cassedy to Charles Clark, September 12, 1864, Charles Clark Correspondence, Mississippi Department of Archives and History; Richmond *Enquirer,* January 16, February 25, 1865.

52. Peter Bruner, *A Slave's Adventures Toward Freedom: Not Fiction, but the True Story of a Struggle* (Oxford, OH: no publisher, 1918), 38–39.

53. Berlin et al., *Destruction of Slavery,* 94–95.

54. E. D. Macnair to Josiah Collins, June 16, 1863, Josiah Collins Papers, North Carolina State Archives.

55. William Elliott to William, August 25, 1862, Elliott and Gonzales Family Papers.

56. Bruner, *Slave's Adventures,* 38–40.

57. Robert A. Taylor, *Rebel Storehouse: Florida in the Confederate Economy* (Tuscaloosa: University of Alabama Press, 1995), 84; Ira Berlin, et al., eds., *The Black Military Experience* (Cambridge: Cambridge University Press, 1982), 237–38; H. Cassedy to Charles Clark, September 12, 1864, Clark Correspondence; James L. Roark, *Masters Without Slaves: Southern Planters in the Civil War and Reconstruction* (New York: W. W. Norton, 1977), 74.

58. Louis Hughes, *Thirty Years a Slave: From Bondage to Freedom* (Milwaukee, WI: South Side Printing, 1897), 154–55.

59. Petition of Samuel Wolf, J. Cerf, and H. Hiller, August 3, 1864, in *Race, Slavery, and Free Blacks: Series I, Petitions to Southern Legislatures, 1777–1867* (microfilm, Bethesda: University Publications of America, 1999), reel 3.

60. Columbus *Daily Columbus Enquirer,* February 22, 1861, quoting Harris County *Enterprise.*

61. Baltimore *Sun,* May 28, September 30, 1861, April 27, 1863; Columbus *Daily Columbus Enquirer,* May 22, 1861, August 28, 1864; New Orleans *Daily True Delta,* August 9, October 3, 1861; Savannah *Daily Morning News,* June 9, 1862; Chattanooga *Daily Rebel,* October 4, 1862; Raleigh *Weekly Register,* September 9, 1863; Jackson *Daily Mississippian,* July 6, 1864; Winthrop D. Jordan, *Tumult and Silence at Second Creek: An Inquiry into a Civil War Slave Conspiracy* (Baton Rouge: Louisiana State University Press, 1993), passim.

62. Columbus *Daily Columbus Enquirer,* February 22, 1861, quoting Harris County *Enterprise.*

63. Columbus *Daily Columbus Enquirer,* March 2, 1861, quoting Harris County *Enterprise.*

64. Petition of Samuel Wolf, J. Cerf, and H. Hiller, August 3, 1864, in *Race, Slavery, and Free Blacks: Series I,* reel 3.

65. Jackson *Daily Mississippian,* July 6, 1864.

66. Rawick, *American Slave,* Orig. Series, 14(Pt. 1): 136.

67. James Marten, *The Children's Civil War* (Chapel Hill: University of North Carolina Press, 1998), 137.

68. C. Alice Ready Diary, March 23, 24, 1862, Southern Historical Collection, University of North Carolina, Chapel Hill.

69. Hardy Hardison to Josiah Collins, March 27, 1863, Collins Papers.

70. Wadley Diary, August 27, 1863.

71. Blakey, Lainhart, and Stephens, *Rose Cottage Chronicles,* 163; Jacqueline Glass Campbell, *When Sherman Marched North from the Sea: Resistance on the Confederate Home Front* (Chapel Hill: University of North Carolina Press, 2003), 45–46, 66.

72. Benjamin Quarles, *The Negro in the Civil War* (1953; repr., New York: Da Capo Press, 1989), 49–50; Drew Gilpin Faust, *Mothers of Invention: Women of the Slaveholding South in the American Civil War* (Chapel Hill: University of North Carolina Press, 1996), 60–61.

73. Blakey, Lainhart, and Stephens, *Rose Cottage Chronicles,* 23n., 201, 211, 215, 239, 260.

74. John W. Blassingame, *The Slave Community: Plantation Life in the Antebellum South* (1972; 2nd ed., New York: Oxford University Press, 1979), passim; Noralee Frankel, *Freedom's*

Women: Black Women and Families in Civil War Era Mississippi (Bloomington: Indiana University Press, 1999), 19–22, 161–62.

75. Mattaponi Baptist Church (King and Queen County, Virginia) Minute Book, August 9, 1862, Virginia State Library and Archives.

76. J. S. Dunn to H. Blackmon, January 5, 1864, Homer Blackmon Papers, Perkins Library, Duke University.

CHAPTER 2

1. The foregoing survey of Southern agriculture and the slaves' role in it is drawn from Lewis C. Gray, *History of Agriculture in the Southern United States to 1860* (2 vols., Washington, D.C.: Carnegie Institution, 1933); Sam B. Hilliard, *Hog Meat and Hoecake: Food Supply in the Old South, 1840–1860* (Carbondale: Southern Illinois University Press, 1972); Paul W. Gates, *Agriculture and the Civil War* (New York: Knopf, 1965); John Solomon Otto, *Southern Agriculture During the Civil War Era, 1860–1880* (Westport, CT: Greenwood Press, 1994); Kenneth M. Stampp, *The Peculiar Institution: Slavery in the Ante-Bellum South* (New York: Vintage Books, 1956); and Eugene D. Genovese, *Roll, Jordan, Roll: The World the Slaves Made* (New York: Vintage Books, 1974).

2. Racine, *Piedmont Farmer,* 1–5, 190–92.

3. Rawick, *American Slave,* Orig. Series, 4(Pt. 2): 131.

4. Rawick, *American Slave,* Orig. Series, 3(Pt. 4): 92.

5. Rawick, *American Slave,* Orig. Series, 14(Pt. 1): 279.

6. Gates, *Agriculture and the Civil War,* 15–22; Roark, *Masters Without Slaves,* 41.

7. Otto, *Southern Agriculture,* 34; Gates, *Agriculture and the Civil War,* 77, 103–4; Roark, *Masters Without Slaves,* 78–79.

8. Rawick, *American Slave,* Suppl. Series Two, 7(Pt. 6): 2816.

9. Rawick, *American Slave,* Orig. Series, 3(Pt. 3): 20.

10. Rawick, *American Slave,* Orig. Series, 4(Pt. 1): 14–15, Suppl. Series Two, 2(Pt. 1): 50–51; Savannah *Daily Morning News,* June 9, 1862.

11. James M. McPherson, *Battle Cry of Freedom: The Civil War Era* (New York: Oxford University Press, 1988), 611–12.

12. Rawick, *American Slave,* Orig. Series, 15(Pt. 2): 66–67.

13. Racine, *Piedmont Farmer,* 267–68.

14. Rawick, *American Slave,* Orig. Series, 4(Pt. 2): 77–78.

15. Blakey, Lainhart, and Stephens, *Rose Cottage Chronicles,* 200, 226, 260.

16. Rawick, *American Slave,* Suppl. Series Two, 6(Pt. 5): 1962–63.

17. John Rozier, ed., *The Granite Farm Letters: The Civil War Correspondence of Edgeworth and Sallie Bird* (Athens: University of Georgia Press, 1988), 127, 133.

18. Steven Deyle, *Carry Me Back: The Domestic Slave Trade in American Life* (Oxford: Oxford University Press, 2005).

19. Bell Irvin Wiley, *Southern Negroes, 1861–1865* (New Haven, CT: Yale University Press, 1938), 87–93.

20. Jackson *Daily Southern Crisis,* January 19, 1863, quoting Staunton (Virginia) *Spectator.*

21. Fayetteville (North Carolina) *Observer,* January 5, 1865.

22. Jason Niles Diary, November 13, 1862, Southern Homefront 1861–1865 Collection, Documenting the American South Digital Library, University of North Carolina, Chapel Hill, http://www.docsouth.unc.edu (accessed December 10, 2007).

23. Fayetteville *Observer,* April 13, 1863, quoting Galveston *News.*

24. Richmond *Enquirer,* October 18, 1862.

25. Rawick, *American Slave,* Orig. Series, 7(Pt. 1): 289–90.

26. Stampp, *Peculiar Institution,* 67–72; John C. Inscoe and Gordon B. McKinney, *The Heart of Confederate Appalachia: Western North Carolina in the Civil War* (Chapel Hill: University of North Carolina Press, 2000), 211–14; petition of Reese Price to Mississippi legislature, November 1863, in *Race, Slavery and Free Blacks: Series I,* reel 3.

27. Erwin Diary, July 4, 1864.

28. Dimond and Hattaway, *Letters from Forest Place,* 239.

29. Cushing Biggs Hassell Diary, August 4, 1863, Southern Historical Collection, University of North Carolina, Chapel Hill.

30. Racine, *Piedmont Farmer,* 215.

31. Wadley Diary, December 26, 1862, March 30, 1863.

32. Natchez *Daily Courier,* May 5, 1863.

33. Kimberly Harrison, *Maryland Bride in the Deep South: The Civil War Diary of Priscilla Bond* (Baton Rouge: Louisiana State University Press, 2006), 213.

34. Virginia Ingraham Burr, ed., *The Secret Eye: The Journal of Ella Gertrude Clanton Thomas, 1848–1889* (Chapel Hill: University of North Carolina Press, 1990), 215–16.

35. Parker, *Recollections of Slavery Times,* 78–80.

36. Rawick, *American Slave,* Orig. Series, 9(Pt. 4): 180–81.

37. Rawick, *American Slave,* Suppl. Series Two, 2(Pt. 1): 252.

38. Rawick, *American Slave,* Orig. Series, 12(Pt. 1): 187.

39. Rawick, *American Slave,* Suppl. Series Two, 5(Pt. 4): 1840–41.

40. Rawick, *American Slave,* Suppl. Series Two, 3(Pt. 2): 684.

41. Session minutes, October 12, 1863, Union Church Presbyterian Church Records, Mississippi Department of Archives and History.

42. Academy Baptist Church Minute Book, May 1862, Mississippi Department of Archives and History.

43. John F. Marszalek, ed., *The Diary of Miss Emma Holmes, 1861–1866* (Baton Rouge: Louisiana State University Press, 1979), 427–28.

44. Hughes, *Thirty Years a Slave,* 53–54, 90–91, 147, 174.

45. Stampp, *Peculiar Institution,* 160; Malet, *Errand to the South,* 70.

46. Eliza Frances Andrews, *The War-time Journal of a Georgia Girl, 1864–1865* (New York: D. Appleton, 1908), 89–91, 101.

47. Albert J. Raboteau, *Slave Religion: The "Invisible Institution" in the Antebellum South* (Oxford: Oxford University Press, 1978), 223–24, 225–26; Fayetteville *Observer,* November 12, 1863.

48. Richard L. Troutman, ed., *The Heavens Are Weeping: The Diaries of George Richard Browder, 1852–1886* (Grand Rapids, MI: Zonervan Publishing House, 1987), 161–64.

49. Mary Elizabeth Massey, *Ersatz in the Confederacy: Shortages and Substitutes on the Southern Homefront* (1952; repr., Columbia: University of South Carolina Press, 1993), chaps. 1 and 2.

50. Ibid., passim, esp. 3–5, 26–27, 79–80; Wiley, *Southern Negroes,* 48; Mohr, *On the Threshold of Freedom,* 210–11, 213.

51. Judith N. McArthur and Orville Vernon Burton, *"A Gentleman and an Officer": A Military and Social History of James B. Griffin's Civil War* (New York: Oxford University Press, 1996), 186–87.

52. Dimond and Hattaway, *Letters from Forest Place,* 288.

53. Albert V. House, Jr., "Deterioration of a Georgia Rice Plantation During Four Years of Civil War," *Journal of Southern History* 9(1943): 108.

54. Ash, *When the Yankees Came,* 99–101.

55. John Houston Bills Diary, December 26, 1862, Southern Historical Collection, University of North Carolina, Chapel Hill.

56. Rawick, *American Slave,* Orig. Series, 8(Pt. 2):139.

57. Childs, *Private Journal of Ravenel,* 165.

58. Racine, *Piedmont Farmer,* 360.

59. Julia Johnson Fisher Diary, January 1, February 6, 1864, Southern Homefront 1861–1865 Collection, Documenting the American South Digital Library, University of North Carolina, Chapel Hill, http://www.docsouth.unc.edu (accessed December 6, 2007).

60. Houston *Tri-Weekly Telegraph,* January 6, 1864.

61. Rawick, *American Slave,* Suppl. Series One, 8(Pt. 3): 818–19; Marszalek, *Diary of Miss Emma Holmes,* 215.

62. Roark, *Masters Without Slaves,* 83; Hassell Diary, February 28, 1865.

63. Childs, *Private Journal of Ravenel,* 210–11.

64. Robert Manson Myers, ed., *The Children of Pride: A True Story of Georgia and the Civil War* (New Haven, CT: Yale University Press, 1972), 878.

65. Troutman, *Heavens Are Weeping,* 131, 140–41, 145, 178.

66. Henry L. Swint, ed., *Dear Ones at Home: Letters from Contraband Camps* (Nashville: Vanderbilt University Press, 1966), 42.

67. Rawick, *American Slave,* Suppl. Series Two, 2(Pt. 1): 402–3.

68. Rawick, *American Slave,* Orig. Series, 14(Pt. 1): 157.

69. Rawick, *American Slave,* Orig. Series, 4(Pt. 1): 15.

70. Parker, *Recollections of Slavery Times,* 84.

71. Racine, *Piedmont Farmer,* 340–41.

72. Rawick, *American Slave,* Suppl. Series Two, 8(Pt. 7): 3387.

73. Myers, *Children of Pride,* 1062–63.

74. Troutman, *Heavens Are Weeping,* 136–37.

75. Rawick, *American Slave,* Suppl. Series Two, 2(Pt. 1): 51–53, Orig. Series, 4(Pt. 1): 15–16.

76. Racine, *Piedmont Farmer,* 351.

77. Sister to Emmie, n.d. (fall 1862), Elliott and Gonzales Family Papers.

78. Racine, *Piedmont Farmer,* 267–68, 269, 274, 355, 357–58, 365.

79. Ibid., 367.

80. Faust, *Mothers of Invention,* 63–70; Mohr, *On the Threshold of Freedom,* 220–32.

81. Henry Jones to J. R. Donnell, December 30, 1862, Bryan Family Papers, Perkins Library, Duke University.

82. Colin Clarke to Maxwell Clarke, September 14, 1862, September 20, 1863, Maxwell Troax Clarke Papers, Southern Historical Collection, University of North Carolina, Chapel Hill.

83. Racine, *Piedmont Farmer,* 235.

84. Rawick, *American Slave,* Suppl. Series Two, 2(Pt. 1): 51–53.

85. Hassell Diary, February 3, 28, 1865.

86. Ibid., May 8, 1865.

87. Racine, *Piedmont Farmer,* 370–78.

CHAPTER 3

1. Wiley, *Southern Negroes,* 134; Rawick, *American Slave,* Suppl. Series Two, 4(Pt. 3): 1177.

2. McArthur and Burton, *"A Gentleman and an Officer,"* 186.

3. Wiley, *Southern Negroes,* 135–37.

4. Rawick, *American Slave,* Suppl. Series Two, 7(Pt. 6): 2472–73.

5. Rawick, *American Slave,* Suppl. Series Two, 3(Pt. 2): 875–76.

6. Rawick, *American Slave,* Suppl. Series Two, 3(Pt. 2): 684.

7. Rawick, *American Slave,* Suppl. Series Two, 9(Pt. 8): 3610–23.

8. McArthur and Burton, *"A Gentleman and an Officer,"* 221.

9. Charleston *Courier Tri-Weekly,* September 30, 1862; James H. Brewer, *The Confederate Negro: Virginia's Craftsmen and Military Laborers, 1861–1865* (Durham, NC: Duke University Press, 1969), 17–30; Taylor, *Rebel Storehouse,* 83–84; William Warren Rogers, Jr., *Confederate Home Front: Montgomery During the Civil War* (Tuscaloosa: University of Alabama Press, 1999), 57.

10. Mohr, *On the Threshold of Freedom,* 136; Joseph T. Glatthaar, *General Lee's Army: From Victory to Collapse* (New York: Free Press, 2008), 309, 312; Ervin L. Jordan, Jr., *Black Confederates and Afro-Yankees in Civil War Virginia* (Charlottesville: University Press of Virginia, 1995), 190, 191, 222–26; Wiley, *Southern Negroes,* 139–40; Quarles, *Negro in the Civil War,* 37–41; Arthur W. Bergeron, Jr., *Confederate Mobile* (Jackson: University Press of Mississippi, 1991), 105–6; Bruce Levine, *Confederate Emancipation: Southern Plans to Free and Arm Slaves During the Civil War* (New York: Oxford University Press, 2005), passim, esp. 140–47.

11. Brewer, *Confederate Negro,* 3–4, 7, 31–73.

12. Ibid., 36–73; Mohr, *On the Threshold of Freedom,* 143–56; Charles B. Dew, *Ironmaker to the Confederacy: Joseph R. Anderson and the Tredegar Iron Works* (New Haven, CT: Yale University Press, 1966), 250; Jordan, *Black Confederates and Afro-Yankees,* 51–54.

13. Payroll of hired slaves, January 1863, Arkadelphia (Arkansas) Arsenal, document 3299, E-56, War Department Collection of Confederate Records, RG 109, National Archives, Washington.

14. Brewer, *Confederate Negro,* 31, 37, 52–53, 60–61; Dew, *Ironmaker to the Confederacy,* 262–63.

15. Brewer, *Confederate Negro,* 60–61; Dew, *Ironmaker to the Confederacy,* 262–63; Mohr, *On the Threshold of Freedom,* 179–86.

16. Stephen V. Ash, *A Year in the South: Four Lives in 1865* (New York: Palgrave Macmillan, 2002), 19–24; George E. Buker, *Blockaders, Refugees, and Contrabands: Civil War on Florida's Gulf Coast, 1861–1865* (Tuscaloosa: University of Alabama Press, 1993), 46–49; Jordan, *Black Confederates and Afro-Yankees,* 53–54.

17. Brewer, *Confederate Negro,* 35, 74–94; Mohr, *On the Threshold of Freedom,* 136–42.

18. Nancy Schurr, "Inside the Confederate Hospital: Community and Conflict During the Civil War" (Ph.D. diss., University of Tennessee, 2004), 10, 144–70; Brewer, *Confederate Negro,* 95–130; Mohr, *On the Threshold of Freedom,* 128–35.

19. Rawick, *American Slave,* Suppl. Series Two, 8(Pt. 7): 3230–31.

20. Berlin et al., *Destruction of Slavery,* 664–72; Brewer, *Confederate Negro,* 82, 131–64.

21. Litwack, *Been in the Storm,* 37–38; Childs, *Private Journal of Ravenel,* 46, 50; Berlin et al., *Destruction of Slavery,* 668–70; Brewer, *Confederate Negro,* 6–14, 139–40.

22. Racine, *Piedmont Farmer,* 329.

23. Fonsylvania Plantation Journal, February 20, 1863, Mississippi Department of Archives and History; Brewer, *Confederate Negro,* 142–43, 150; Mohr, *On the Threshold of Freedom,* 124, 128; Malcolm C. McMillan, *The Disintegration of a Confederate State: Three Governors and Alabama's Wartime Home Front, 1861–1865* (Macon, GA: Mercer University Press, 1986), 54, 111.

24. Brewer, *Confederate Negro,* 135–36, 153–54.

25. Rawick, *American Slave,* Orig. Series, 9(Pt. 4): 181–82.

26. Bergeron, *Confederate Mobile,* 110–11.

27. Frontis W. Johnston and Joe A. Mobley, eds., *The Papers of Zebulon Baird Vance* (2 vols. to date, Raleigh: North Carolina Division of Archives and History, 1963–), 2: 95–96; Berlin et al., *Destruction of Slavery,* 713–14, 728–29; Litwack, *Been in the Storm,* 39.

28. Petition of Reese Price to Mississippi legislature, November 1863, in *Race, Slavery and Free Blacks: Series I,* reel 3.

29. Stroyer, *My Life in the South,* 36–38.

30. Berlin et al., *Destruction of Slavery,* 728–29.

31. Charleston *Courier Tri-Weekly,* February 8, 1862; Richmond *Daily Examiner,* November 24, 1864.

32. Dimond and Hattaway, *Letters from Forest Place,* 301, 303.

33. Glatthaar, *General Lee's Army,* 309, 311; Mohr, *On the Threshold of Freedom,* 172–75.

34. Ira Berlin, *Slaves Without Masters: The Free Negro in the Antebellum South* (1974; repr., New York: Vintage Books, 1976), 176; Mohr, *On the Threshold of Freedom,* 190–96.

35. Rawick, *American Slave,* Suppl. Series Two, 8(Pt. 7): 3231.

36. Isabella Middleton Leland, ed., "Middleton Correspondence, 1861–1865," *South Carolina Historical Magazine,* 63(1962): 61.

37. Fayetteville *Observer,* November 24, 1862.

38. Richard C. Wade, *Slavery in the Cities: The South, 1820–1860* (Oxford: Oxford University Press, 1964), 48–50; petition of Madison County citizens to Mississippi legislature, 1862, in *Race, Slavery, and Free Blacks: Series I,* reel 3; Charleston *Courier Tri-Weekly,* September 30, 1862.

39. Steven Elliott Tripp, *Yankee Town, Southern City: Race and Class Relations in Civil War Lynchburg* (New York: New York University Press, 1997), 153.

40. Richmond *Daily Examiner,* October 6, 1863, February 3, 1864; Richmond *Whig & Public Advertiser,* May 17, 1864; Chattanooga *Daily Rebel,* November 19, 1862, quoting Richmond *Examiner.*

41. Wade, *Slavery in the Cities,* 161–72, 271–72; Berlin, *Slaves Without Masters,* 173, 285–303.

42. Savannah *Daily Morning News,* June 1, 1861, May 30, June 1, 1863; Jacqueline Jones, *Saving Savannah: The City and the Civil War* (New York: Alfred A. Knopf, 2008), 58–59; Jackson *Weekly Mississippian,* October 30, 1861; Jackson *Daily Mississippian,* April 15, 1863; Houston *Tri-Weekly Telegraph,* May 18, 1863.

43. Wade, *Slavery in the Cities,* 84–90; Montgomery *Daily Mail,* January 6, 1865.

44. Columbus *Daily Columbus Enquirer,* August 12, 1862.

45. Houston *Tri-Weekly Telegraph,* May 18, 1863.

46. Richmond *Daily Examiner,* October 6, 1863.

47. Fayetteville *Observer,* September 19, 1864, quoting Richmond *Examiner.*

48. Jackson *Daily Southern Crisis,* March 13, 1863.

49. Petition of Madison County citizens to Mississippi legislature, 1862, in *Race, Slavery, and Free Blacks: Series I,* reel 3.

50. Montgomery *Daily Mail,* January 6, 1865.

51. Mohr, *On the Threshold of Freedom,* 207.

52. Richmond *Daily Examiner,* October 21, 1864.

53. Berlin, *Slaves Without Masters,* 136–37, 176.

54. Ibid., passim.

55. Baltimore *Sun,* January 31, February 4, 1861; Fayetteville *Observer,* February 11, April 1, 1861.

56. Raleigh *Daily Register,* April 24, 1861.

57. Litwack, *Been in the Storm,* 29; Williams, *Rich Man's War,* 159.

58. Jackson *Weekly Mississippian,* August 7, 1861.

59. Berlin et al., *Destruction of Slavery,* 678–79; Brewer, *Confederate Negro,* 6–7, 12–13, 134–40, 145.

60. Fayetteville *Observer,* October 21, 1861.

61. Johnston and Mobley, *Papers of Vance,* 2:228.

62. Jordan, *Black Confederates and Afro-Yankees,* 203–4.

63. Berlin et al., *Destruction of Slavery,* 762; Brewer, *Confederate Negro,* 13.

64. Richmond *Daily Examiner,* November 19, 1863; Raleigh *Weekly Register,* October 16, 1861.

65. Brewer, *Confederate Negro,* passim, esp. 7, 57, 89; Schurr, "Inside the Confederate Hospital," 166–67.

66. Brewer, *Confederate Negro,* 19, 21–22; Tinsley Lee Spraggins, "Mobilization of Negro Labor for the Department of Virginia and North Carolina," *North Carolina Historical Review,* 24(1947): 168–69.

67. Brewer, *Confederate Negro,* 7, 134–35; Savannah *Daily Morning News,* June 6, 11, 1861, January 3, March 25, 1862; Fayetteville *Observer,* November 24, 1862, quoting Savannah *Republican.*

68. New Orleans *Daily True Delta,* April 25, 1861, quoting Abbeville (South Carolina) *Banner;* Camden (South Carolina) *Confederate,* July 18, 1862; Savannah *Daily Morning News,* March 28, 1862.

69. Jackson *Weekly Mississippian,* October 30, 1861.

70. New Orleans *Daily True Delta,* April 25, 1861, quoting Abbeville *Banner.*

71. Fayetteville *Observer,* November 24, 1862, quoting Savannah *Republican.*

72. Litwack, *Been in the Storm,* 16–17, 42; Mohr, *On the Threshold of Freedom,* 64–67.

73. Berlin et al., *Black Military Experience,* 313.

74. Berlin et al., *Destruction of Slavery,* 675–76.

75. Fayetteville *Observer,* January 14, 1861; Baltimore *Sun,* March 28, 1861; Natchez *Weekly Courier,* September 11, 1861.

76. New Orleans *Daily True Delta,* October 15, 1861; Raleigh *Daily Register,* November 27, 1861; House, "Deterioration of a Georgia Rice Plantation," 104; Fayetteville *Observer,* February 20, December 15, 1862, June 8, 1863; Richmond *Enquirer,* October 18, 1862; Mary Milling to husband, November 20, 1863, James S. Milling Papers, Southern Homefront 1861–1865 Collection, Documenting the American South Digital Library, University of North Carolina, Chapel Hill, http://www.docsouth.unc.edu (accessed December 10, 2007); statement of A. B. Thornton, June 8, 1864, in *War of the Rebellion,* Series One, 38(Pt. 4): 438, 22(Pt. 2): 990; Louis M. De Saussure Plantation Record, April 14, 1862, Southern Historical Collection, University of North Carolina, Chapel Hill.

77. Myers, *Children of Pride,* 998; Rawick, *American Slave,* Orig. Series, 14(Pt. 1): 400.

78. Fayetteville *Observer,* June 8, 1863; Myers, *Children of Pride,* 858; Rawick, *American Slave,* Orig. Series, 7(Pt. 1): 215–21.

79. Erwin Diary, December 20–24, 1862.

80. Rawick, *American Slave,* Orig. Series, 4(Pt. 1): 108.

81. Leslie A. Schwalm, *A Hard Fight for We: Women's Transition from Slavery to Freedom in South Carolina* (Urbana: University of Illinois Press, 1997), 108–11; Meta Morris Grimball Journal, November 27, 1862, First-Person Narratives of the American South Collection, Documenting the American South Digital Library, University of North Carolina, Chapel Hill, http://www.docsouth.unc.edu (accessed December 7, 2007); Childs, *Private Journal of Ravenel,* 103.

82. Rawick, *American Slave,* Orig. Series, 14(Pt. 1): 400.

83. Frankel, *Freedom's Women,* 17–18.

84. Agnew Diary, May 12, 13, 1863; John A. Downey to L. D. Burwell, February 24, 1863, Samuel Smith Downey Papers, Perkins Library, Duke University; Rawick, *American Slave,* Orig. Series, 6(Pt. 1): 181–82.

85. Myers, *Children of Pride,* 973, 976–79, 982, 985–87; Malet, *Errand to the South,* 96–97; Rawick, *American Slave,* Orig. Series, 7(Pt. 1): 221–22, Suppl. Series One, 12(Pt. 1): 173–74.

86. Fayetteville *Observer,* April 21, 1862; Myers, *Children of Pride,* 1129, 1133, 1140, 1145, 1162, 1178.

87. Richmond *Enquirer,* October 18, 1862.

88. Rawick, *American Slave,* Orig. Series, 6(Pt. 1): 181–82.

CHAPTER 4

1. The foregoing discussion of Union emancipation policy is drawn from Berlin et al., *Destruction of Slavery,* 14–37, and Allen C. Guelzo, *Lincoln's Emancipation Proclamation: The End of Slavery in America* (New York: Simon and Schuster, 2004), passim.

2. Ash, *When the Yankees Came,* 150; Berlin et al., *Destruction of Slavery,* 132–33.

3. Report of John Kennett, March 8, 1862, in *War of the Rebellion,* Series One, 10(Pt. 1): 6.

4. O. M. Mitchell to E. M. Stanton, May 4, 1862, in *War of the Rebellion,* Series One, 10(Pt. 2): 162.

5. John Beatty, *Memoirs of a Volunteer, 1861–1863* (New York: W. W. Norton, 1946.

6. Betty Herndon Maury Diary, May 16, June 22, 1862, Library of Congress.

7. Bills Diary, July 30, 1862.

8. Robert H. Cartmell Diary, August 20, November 13, 1862, Tennessee State Library and Archives.

9. Fonsylvania Plantation Journal, May 6–June 6, 1863.

10. Nashville *Dispatch,* July 28, 1863.

11. Lovell H. Rousseau to W. D. Whipple, January 30, 1864, in *War of the Rebellion,* Series One, 32(Pt. 2): 268.

12. John Fitch, *Annals of the Army of the Cumberland* (Philadelphia: J. B. Lippincott, 1864), 270.

13. William C. Harris, *With Charity for All: Lincoln and the Restoration of the Union* (Lexington: University Press of Kentucky, 1997), passim.

14. Baltimore *Sun,* January 7, 1863; Ira Berlin, et al., eds., *The Wartime Genesis of Free Labor: The Lower South* (Cambridge: Cambridge University Press, 1990), 87–89.

15. Berlin et al., *Destruction of Slavery,* 210–11.

16. Mary Fielding Diary, August 14, 1862, Alabama Department of Archives and History.

17. Frederick D. Williams, ed., *The Wild Life of the Army: Civil War Letters of James A. Garfield* (East Lansing: Michigan State College Press, 1964), 257.

18. R. L. Dixon to Harry Dixon, March 6, 1863, Harry St. John Dixon Papers, Southern Historical Collection, University of North Carolina, Chapel Hill.

19. Report of Frank P. Blair, Jr., May 31, 1863, in *War of the Rebellion,* Series One, 24(Pt. 2): 436.

20. Richard Harwell and Philip N. Racine, eds., *The Fiery Trail: A Union Officer's Account of Sherman's Last Campaigns* (Knoxville: University of Tennessee Press, 1986), 170, 184.

21. Henry Hitchcock Diary, November 18, 1864, Henry Hitchcock Papers, Library of Congress.

22. Amanda Worthington Diary, April 23, 24, 1863, Worthington Family Papers, Mississippi Department of Archives and History.

23. Lynda J. Morgan, *Emancipation in Virginia's Tobacco Belt, 1850–1870* (Athens: University of Georgia Press, 1992), 113–14; Columbus *Daily Columbus Enquirer,* September 15, 1862.

24. Glatthaar, *General Lee's Army,* 312–13; Berlin et al., *Destruction of Slavery,* 565.

25. McArthur and Burton, *"A Gentleman and an Officer,"* 221.

26. Mohr, *On the Threshold of Freedom,* 72–74.

27. Rawick, *American Slave,* Orig. Series, 10(Pt. 6): 337–38.

28. Parker, *Recollections of Slavery Times,* 85–86.

29. Ibid., 86–89.

30. Swint, *Dear Ones at Home,* 42.

31. Hiram Yugee to William Smith, November 2, 1864, Virginia Executive Papers, Virginia State Library and Archives.

32. Rawick, *American Slave,* Orig. Series, 8(Pt. 1): 168–69.

33. Stephen V. Ash, *Firebrand of Liberty: The Story of Two Black Regiments That Changed the Course of the Civil War* (New York: W. W. Norton, 2008), 38.

34. "Letters of Dr. Seth Rogers, 1862, 1863," *Massachusetts Historical Society Proceedings* 43(1910): 362–63.

35. Ibid., 363–64.

36. Thomas Wentworth Higginson, *Army Life in a Black Regiment* (1870; repr., New York: Collier Books, 1962), 78–79; Ash, *Firebrand of Liberty,* 61.

37. Berlin et al., *Destruction of Slavery,* 333–34, 361–62, 499–500.

38. Baltimore *Sun,* September 16, 1863.

39. Berlin et al., *Destruction of Slavery,* 372–76.

40. Ibid., 565–66.

41. Ibid., 376–77.

42. Berlin et al., eds., *The Wartime Genesis of Free Labor: The Upper South* (Cambridge: Cambridge University Press, 1993), 608–10.

43. Berlin et al., *Destruction of Slavery,* 568–70.

44. Ibid., 566.

45. Baltimore *Sun,* November 15, 1861, March 25, May 12, June 28, 1862; Berlin et al., *Destruction of Slavery,* 159–67.

46. Baltimore *Sun,* June 23, 1862.

47. Berlin et al., *Destruction of Slavery,* 331–41, 395–412, 493–518; Victor B. Howard, *Black Liberation in Kentucky: Emancipation and Freedom, 1862–1884* (Lexington: University Press of Kentucky, 1983), 16–19, 51–52, 57–58, 63–64; Berlin et al., *Wartime Genesis,* 608–10; Barbara Jeanne Fields, *Slavery and Freedom on the Middle Ground: Maryland During the Nineteenth Century* (New Haven, CT: Yale University Press, 1985), 124–28; Berlin et al., *Black Military Experience,* 183–97.

48. Berlin et al., *Black Military Experience,* 194, 196; Fields, *Slavery and Freedom on the Middle Ground,* 126; Bruce, *New Man,* 107.

49. Baltimore *Sun,* November 11, 1863.

50. Baltimore *Sun,* September 30, 1863.

51. Baltimore *Sun,* October 24, 1863.

52. Baltimore *Sun,* March 25, 1864.

53. Baltimore *Sun,* November 30, 1864, quoting Louisville *Journal.*

54. Troutman, *Heavens Are Weeping,* 174, 175, 179–80, 181.

55. Bruce, *New Man,* 102, 107.

56. Berlin et al., *Wartime Genesis: Upper South,* 612–13.

57. Berlin et al., *Black Military Experience,* 196–97.

58. Charles Lewis Wagandt, *The Mighty Revolution: Negro Emancipation in Maryland, 1862–1864* (Baltimore, MD: Johns Hopkins University Press, 1964), chaps. 14–16; Berlin et al., *Destruction of Slavery,* 22, 53, 340–41, 412, 493, 515–18; Berlin et al., *Wartime Genesis: Upper South,* 73.

59. University of Virginia Library Historical Census Browser, 1860 population statistics; Louis S. Gerteis, *From Contraband to Freedman: Federal Policy Toward Southern Blacks, 1861–1865* (Westport, CT: Greenwood Press, 1973), 193–94.

60. Jane Washington to George A. Washington, August 8, 1864, Washington Family Papers, Tennessee State Library and Archives.

61. Report of William A. Haw, April 3, 1862, in *War of the Rebellion,* Series One, 10 (Pt. 1):82.

62. Ash, *Firebrand of Liberty,* 128–29.

63. Frank R. Levstik, ed., "A Journey Among the Contrabands: The Diary of Walter Totten Carpenter," *Indiana Magazine of History* 73(1977): 222.

CHAPTER 5

1. Girard Phelps to Josiah Collins, March 14, 1863, Collins Papers.

2. Frank to Ann, April 13, 1863, Anonymous Civil War Letter, Special Collections, Louisiana State University.

3. Troutman, *Heavens Are Weeping,* 179, 186, 194.

4. Berlin et al., *Wartime Genesis: Lower South,* 785.

5. Ibid., 35–40, 46–61, 64–72, 75–77; John Cimprich, *Slavery's End in Tennessee, 1861–1865* (University of Alabama Press, 1985), 65–70; Gerteis, *From Contraband to Freedman,* 84–85, 157–58, and passim.

6. Janet Sharp Hermann, *The Pursuit of a Dream* (New York: Oxford University Press, 1981), chaps. 2 and 3.

7. Berlin et al., *Wartime Genesis: Lower South,* 111–12, 338–40.

8. *Nimrod Porter Journal,* February 28, March 7, 21, 24, 25, 1865, Southern Historical Collection, University of North Carolina, Chapel Hill.

9. R. P. Gaillard to Edward Bigelow, February 3, 1865, E-1488, Vol. IV, Records of U.S. Army Continental Commands, 1821–1920, RG 393, National Archives, Washington.

10. Wilmer Shields to William Mercer, January 25, 1864, William N. Mercer Papers, Special Collections, Louisiana State University.

11. Berlin et al., *Wartime Genesis: Lower South,* 455–56.

12. Ibid., 791.

13. Ibid., 878.

14. Baltimore *Sun,* November 14, 1864.

15. Baltimore *Sun,* November 21, 1864.

16. Baltimore *Sun,* December 15, 1864.

17. Berlin et al., *Wartime Genesis: Upper South,* 494–96, 510–11.

18. Rawick, *American Slave,* Orig. Series, 8(Pt. 1): 169.

19. Fitch, *Annals of the Army,* 270.

20. Berlin et al., *Wartime Genesis: Lower South,* 20–21, 62; Schwalm, *Hard Fight for We,* 99; C. Peter Ripley, *Slaves and Freedmen in Civil War Louisiana* (Baton Rouge: Louisiana State University Press, 1976), 40–42.

21. Berlin et al., *Wartime Genesis: Lower South,* 31–33; Patricia C. Click, *Time Full of Trial: The Roanoke Island Freedmen's Colony, 1862–1867* (Chapel Hill: University of North Carolina Press: 2001), 1–9; Cimprich, *Slavery's End in Tennessee,* 48–59.

22. Berlin et al., *Wartime Genesis: Lower South,* 32, 42–43, 62–64; Frankel, *Freedom's Women,* 35–38; Marten, *Children's Civil War,* 129; Cimprich, *Slavery's End in Tennessee,* 56, 64–65.

23. Cimprich, *Slavery's End in Tennessee,* 46–47; Berlin et al., *Wartime Genesis: Upper South,* 25–26; Alexandria (Virginia) *Gazette,* January 10, 1865.

24. Steven Hahn, *A Nation Under Our Feet: Black Political Struggles in the Rural South from Slavery to the Great Migration* (Cambridge: Belknap Press, 2003), 106–9, 118).

25. Berlin et al., *Black Military Experience,* 811–16.

26. Litwack, *Been in the Storm,* 297.

27. American Freedmen's Inquiry Commission Preliminary and Final Reports, p. 56, File 7, Reel 201, Letters Received by the Adjutant General, RG 94, M619, National Archives, Washington.

28. Dudley Taylor Cornish, *The Sable Arm: Negro Troops in the Union Army, 1861–1865* (1956; repr., New York: W. W. Norton, 1966), passim; John David Smith, "Let Us All Be Grateful That We Have Colored Troops That Will Fight," in *Black Soldiers in Blue: African American Troops in the Civil War Era,* ed. John David Smith (Chapel Hill: University of North Carolina Press, 2002), 1–77; Berlin et al., *Black Military Experience,* 1–16, 37–45; Ash, *Firebrand of Liberty,* 32–34, 200–203.

29. Berlin et al., *Black Military Experience,* 12, 14n.; Ash, *Firebrand of Liberty,* 202; Steven J. Ramold, *Slaves, Sailors, Citizens: African Americans in the Union Navy* (DeKalb: Northern Illinois University Press, 2002), passim.

30. Report of P. F. Stevens, January 27, 1862, in *War of the Rebellion,* Series One, 6: 78–81.

31. Berlin et al., *Destruction of Slavery,* 217.

32. Baltimore *Sun,* January 2, 1863, quoting Washington *Star.*

33. Click, *Time Full of Trial,* 9–10, 14–15, 105–24; Marten, *Children's Civil War,* 132–36; Ripley, *Slaves and Freedmen,* 126–45; Keith P. Wilson, *Campfires of Freedom: The Camp Life of Black Soldiers During the Civil War* (Kent, OH: Kent State University Press, 2002), chap. 4.

34. Nashville *Daily Times and True Union,* April 18, 1864.

35. Ash, *Year in the South,* 56–57.

36. Susie King Taylor, *Reminiscences of My Life in Camp with the 33rd United States Colored Troops, Late 1st S. C. Volunteers* (Boston: no publisher, 1902), 52 and passim.

37. Swint, *Dear Ones at Home,* 144.

38. Berlin et al., *Black Military Experience,* 618–19.

39. Marten, *Children's Civil War,* 136.

40. Litwack, *Been in the Storm,* 229–30; Ripley, *Slaves and Freedmen,* 157.

41. Berlin et al., *Black Military Experience,* 689–90.

42. N. G. Gill to provost marshal, February 19, 1865, E-1488, Vol. IV, Records of U.S. Army Continental Commands.

43. Ash, "Wall Around Slavery," 62; Jordan, *Black Confederates and Afro-Yankees,* 79–81; Richmond *Daily Examiner,* June 21, 1864.

44. Report of Nathan G. Evans, January 25, 1862, in *War of the Rebellion,* Series One, 6: 77–78; report of P. F. Stevens, January 27, 1862, in *War of the Rebellion,* Series One, 6: 78–81; instructions to P. F. Stevens, January 21, 1862, in *War of the Rebellion,* Series One, 6: 81–82.

45. Charleston *Courier Tri-Weekly,* March 18, 1862; J. A. Seddon to E. Kirby Smith, August 3, 1863, in *War of the Rebellion,* Series One, 22(Pt. 2): 953; report of James P. Major, June 30, 1863, in *War of the Rebellion,* Series One, 26(Pt. 1): 218; report of N. B. Buford, August 1, 1864, in *War of the Rebellion,* Series One, 41(Pt. 1): 190–91; Gerteis, *From Contraband to Freedman,* 158.

46. Joseph G. McKee and M. M. Brown to Andrew Johnson, November 3, 1863, in LeRoy P. Graf, Ralph W. Haskins, and Paul H. Bergeron, eds., *The Papers of Andrew Johnson* (16 vols., Knoxville: University of Tennessee Press, 1967–2000), 6: 450–51.

47. Nashville *Dispatch,* December 9, 1863.

48. Joseph G. McKee and M. M. Brown to Andrew Johnson, November 3, 1863, in Graf, Haskins, and Bergeron, *Papers of Andrew Johnson,* 6: 450–51.

49. Cimprich, *Slavery's End in Tennessee,* 46–48.

50. Ibid., 52–59.

51. Berlin et al., *Wartime Genesis: Upper South,* 232.

52. Rawick, *American Slave,* Suppl. Series One, 12(Pt. 1): 390–91.

53. Cimprich, *Slavery's End in Tennessee,* 52–54.

54. Ibid.

55. Frankel, *Freedom's Women,* 38.

56. Cimprich, *Slavery's End in Tennessee,* 57.

57. Ripley, *Slaves and Freedmen,* 42–43; Berlin et al., *Wartime Genesis: Lower South,* 21–23; Berlin et al., *Wartime Genesis: Upper South,* 166, 202–3.

58. Berlin et al., *Wartime Genesis: Upper South,* 231–35.

59. John David Smith and William Cooper, Jr., eds., *A Union Woman in Civil War Kentucky: The Diary of Frances Peter* (Lexington: University Press of Kentucky, 2000), 177.

60. Nashville *Daily Times and True Union,* April 11, 1864.

61. John W. Birdwell to Andrew Johnson, November 4, 1864, in Graf, Haskins, and Bergeron, *Papers of Andrew Johnson,* 7: 265–66.

62. "Documents: Civil War Diary of Jabez T. Cox," *Indiana Magazine of History* 28 (1932): 52.

63. William King Diary, July 5, 24, 27, 1864, Southern Historical Collection, University of North Carolina, Chapel Hill.

64. Alice Williamson Diary, May 2, 3, 4, 6, 1864, Perkins Library, Duke University.

65. Litwack, *Been in the Storm,* 130.

66. Francis Dickins to General Blenker, November 22, 1861, Francis Asbury Dickins Papers, Southern Historical Collection, University of North Carolina, Chapel Hill.

67. Jordan, *Black Confederates and Afro-Yankees,* 133, 353n.49.

68. Litwack, *Been in the Storm,* 130.

69. Berlin et al., *Black Military Experience,* 17–26, 303–12, 483–87.

70. Ibid., 21, 25.

71. Elijah P. Marrs, *Life and History of the Rev. Elijah P. Marrs* (Louisville, KY: Bradley and Gilbert, 1885), 17–21.

72. Ibid., 20–25.

73. Noah Andre Trudeau, *Like Men of War: Black Troops in the Civil War, 1862–1865* (Boston: Little, Brown, 1998), passim, esp. 466.

74. Berlin et al., *Black Military Experience,* 600–601.

EPILOGUE

1. General Orders No. 32, Department of North Carolina, April 27, 1865, in *War of the Rebellion,* Series One, 47(Pt. 3): 331; Ash, *Year in the South,* 124, 127; Litwack, *Been in the Storm,* 184–85.

2. Hassell Diary, April 16–May 16, 1865; Sarah R. Espy Diary, May 6–June 27, 1865, Alabama Department of Archives and History; Litwack, *Been in the Storm,* 187–88.

3. Rawick, *American Slave,* Orig. Series, 4(Pt. 2): 78.

4. Marrs, *Life and History,* 69.

BIBLIOGRAPHICAL ESSAY

During the century following the Civil War, historians who wrote about the conflict paid far more attention to its military and political aspects than to its social aspects. The wartime black experience, in particular, was much neglected. Two notable exceptions are Bell Irvin Wiley's *Southern Negroes, 1861–1865* (1938) and Benjamin Quarles's *The Negro in the Civil War* (1953). Both are still useful, although Quarles focuses primarily on federal policy regarding blacks and on the use of black troops, while Wiley offends modern readers with his patronizing racial attitude.

In the 1960s and 1970s, spurred by the Civil Rights movement and other social, political, and intellectual influences, many historians turned their attention to the "forgotten people" of America's past, particularly blacks. The most comprehensive work on the Southern black Civil War experience to emerge in those decades was Leon F. Litwack's magisterial *Been in the Storm So Long: The Aftermath of Slavery* (1979), about one-third of which deals with the war years and the rest with the early years of Reconstruction.

The thrust of Litwack's war chapters is the dissolution of slavery and the self-emancipation of the slaves. This theme also dominates many other books dealing with the wartime black experience that appeared in the 1960s and 1970s, and many that have appeared since. The war years are portrayed therein as a time of black liberation, or at least of black restlessness and the loosening of the bonds of slavery, even for slaves held deep in the Confederate interior and thus far beyond the reach of the Union army and the Emancipation Proclamation.

General studies embodying this theme include James M. McPherson, *The Negro's Civil War: How American Negroes Felt and Acted During the War for the Union* (1965); James L. Roark, *Masters Without Slaves: Southern Planters in the Civil War and Reconstruction* (1977); Ira Berlin, et al., eds., *The Destruction of Slavery* (1985); Eric Foner, *Reconstruction: America's Unfinished Revolution, 1863–1877* (1988); and Steven Hahn, *A Nation Under Our Feet: Black Political Struggles in the Rural South from Slavery to the Great Migration* (2003). State and regional studies include C. Peter Ripley, *Slaves and Freedmen in Civil War Louisiana* (1976); John Cimprich, *Slavery's End in Tennessee, 1861–1865* (1985); Clarence L. Mohr, *On the Threshold of Freedom: Masters and Slaves in Civil War Georgia* (1986); Stephen V. Ash, *Middle Tennessee Society Transformed, 1860–1870: War and Peace in the Upper South* (1988); and David Williams, *Rich Man's War: Class, Caste, and Confederate Defeat in the Lower Chattahoochee Valley* (1998).

Scholars owe a particular debt to the work of Ira Berlin and his fellow editors of the series titled *Freedom: A Documentary History of Emancipation, 1861–1867,* of which *The Destruction of Slavery* is a part. These volumes contain not only verbatim transcripts of thousands of relevant documents in the National Archives, thoroughly edited and contextualized, but also excellent essays on many aspects of the Southern black wartime experience. They are a treasure trove for historians investigating the subject.

Many of the Freedom series documents record the words of Southern black people themselves. Such firsthand testimony is indispensable for understanding the black wartime experience. Another very valuable source of such testimony is the multivolume series edited by George P. Rawick titled *The American Slave: A Composite Autobiography* (1972–1979). It contains transcripts of thousands of interviews with former slaves, recorded in the 1930s. See also Andrew Ward, *The Slaves' War: The Civil War in the Words of Former Slaves* (2008), and Elizabeth A. Regosin and Donald R. Shaffer, eds., *Voices of Emancipation: Understanding Slavery, the Civil War, and Reconstruction Through the U.S. Pension Bureau Files* (2008). There are, moreover, a number of published memoirs of former slaves that deal extensively with the war years. See especially Elijah P. Marrs, *Life and History of the Rev. Elijah P. Marrs* (1885); Allen Parker, *Recollections of Slavery Times* (1895); Louis Hughes, *Thirty Years a Slave: From Bondage to Freedom* (1897); and Susie King Taylor, *Reminiscences of My Life in Camp with the 33rd United States Colored Troops, Late 1st S.C. Volunteers* (1902).

Understanding the antebellum experience of black Southerners is essential to understanding their wartime experience. Among the many excellent studies of Southern blacks before the war are Kenneth M. Stampp, *The Peculiar Institution: Slavery in the Ante-Bellum South* (1956); Richard C. Wade, *Slavery in the Cities: The South,*

1820–1860 (1964); John W. Blassingame, *The Slave Community: Plantation Life in the Antebellum South* (1972); Eugene D. Genovese, *Roll, Jordan, Roll: The World the Slaves Made* (1974); Ira Berlin, *Slaves Without Masters: The Free Negro in the Antebellum South* (1974); and Herbert G. Gutman, *The Black Family in Slavery and Freedom, 1750–1925* (1976).

The secession of the Southern states was driven primarily by fears over the future of slavery, and it is therefore unsurprising that whites in the seceded states took extraordinary steps to control slaves. What is surprising is that there is no book-length study of this important subject. There are some useful shorter pieces, however, including Armstead L. Robinson, "In the Shadow of Old John Brown: Insurrection Anxiety and Confederate Mobilization, 1861–1863," *Journal of Negro History* 65 (1980); Stephen V. Ash, "A Wall Around Slavery: Safeguarding the Peculiar Institution on the Confederate Periphery, 1861–1865," in *Nineteenth-Century America: Essays in Honor of Paul H. Bergeron,* ed. W. Todd Groce and Stephen V. Ash (2005); and Armstead L. Robinson, *Bitter Fruits of Bondage: The Demise of Slavery and the Collapse of the Confederacy, 1861–1865* (2005), chapter 2.

Even as Southern whites redoubled their efforts to subjugate black men and women, they put many to work for the Confederate war effort. These black factory and railroad and hospital workers, impressed army laborers, army officers' servants, and others are discussed in Charles B. Dew, *Ironmaker to the Confederacy: Joseph R. Anderson and the Tredegar Iron Works* (1966); James H. Brewer, *The Confederate Negro: Virginia's Craftsmen and Military Laborers, 1861–1865* (1969); and Ervin L. Jordan, Jr., *Black Confederates and Afro-Yankees in Civil War Virginia* (1995).

On the late-war recruitment of slaves as Confederate combat soldiers, a subject beyond the scope of this book (as explained in the Preface), see Bruce Levine, *Confederate Emancipation: Southern Plans to Free and Arm Slaves During the Civil War* (2005). On the other significant topic related to slavery in the Confederacy not discussed herein—the movement to reform the institution—see Eugene D. Genovese, *A Consuming Fire: The Fall of the Confederacy in the Mind of the White Christian South* (1998).

Most slaves in the Confederacy remained on farms and plantations, where they were much affected by wartime economic developments and by state and Confederate government policies in support of the war effort. See T. Conn Bryan, *Confederate Georgia* (1953); John Solomon Otto, *Southern Agriculture During the Civil War Era, 1860–1880* (1994); Robert A. Taylor, *Rebel Storehouse: Florida in the Confederate Economy* (1995); John C. Inscoe and Gordon B. McKinney, *The Heart of Confederate Appalachia: Western North Carolina in the Civil War* (2000); and Mark V. Wetherington, *Plain Folk's Fight: The Civil War and Reconstruction in Piney Woods Georgia* (2005).

The urban slave population was likewise much affected by wartime developments. While there is no general study of urban slaves in the Confederacy, a number of books on specific cities address the slaves' experience, along with that of free blacks.

See Kenneth Coleman, *Confederate Athens* (1967); Emory M. Thomas, *The Confederate State of Richmond: A Biography of the Capital* (1971); Arthur W. Bergeron, Jr., *Confederate Mobile* (1991); Steven Elliott Tripp, *Yankee Town, Southern City: Race and Class Relations in Civil War Lynchburg* (1997); William Warren Rogers, Jr., *Confederate Home Front: Montgomery During the Civil War* (1999); and Jacqueline Jones, *Saving Savannah: The City and the Civil War* (2008).

Slaves in Confederate regions invaded and held by the Union army fared very differently from those remaining within Confederate lines. The complex evolution of federal policy toward slavery in occupied areas is explained in William C. Harris, *With Charity for All: Lincoln and the Restoration of the Union* (1997), and Allen C. Guelzo, *Lincoln's Emancipation Proclamation: The End of Slavery in America* (2004). How the slaves there secured their freedom before and after the Emancipation Proclamation is discussed in Berlin, *Destruction of Slavery*, and Stephen V. Ash, *When the Yankees Came: Conflict and Chaos in the Occupied South, 1861–1865* (1995).

A good deal has been written about the contraband camps and free-labor plantations, where many freed slaves lived and worked during the war, and about the freed people's relations with the Yankee missionaries, federal officials, and planters there. See especially Willie Lee Rose, *Rehearsal for Reconstruction: The Port Royal Experiment* (1964); Louis S. Gerteis, *From Contraband to Freedman: Federal Policy Toward Southern Blacks, 1861–1865* (1973); Robert Francis Engs, *Freedom's First Generation: Black Hampton, Virginia, 1861–1890* (1979); Lawrence N. Powell, *New Masters: Northern Planters During the Civil War and Reconstruction* (1980); Janet Sharp Hermann, *The Pursuit of Dream* (1981) (on the Davis Bend experiment); Ira Berlin, et al., eds., *The Wartime Genesis of Free Labor: The Lower South* (1990) and *The Wartime Genesis of Free Labor: The Upper South* (1993) (volumes in the Freedom series); and Patricia C. Click, *Time Full of Trial: The Roanoke Island Freedmen's Colony, 1862–1867* (2001).

The story of blacks in the Border states during the war has not been fully told. There is no general study of the subject, and no book-length state studies except for Maryland and Kentucky: see Charles Lewis Wagandt, *The Mighty Revolution: Negro Emancipation in Maryland, 1862–1864* (1964); Victor B. Howard, *Black Liberation in Kentucky: Emancipation and Freedom, 1862–1884* (1983); and Barbara Jeanne Fields, *Slavery and Freedom on the Middle Ground: Maryland During the Nineteenth Century* (1985). The Freedom series volumes, however, offer valuable essays and numerous documents relating to all the Border states.

The black men who served in the Union Army attracted considerable attention from historians even before the black Civil War experience in general became a subject of interest. See, in addition to the Quarles book noted previously, George W. Williams, *A History of the Negro Troops in the War of the Rebellion, 1861–1865* (1888), and Dudley Taylor Cornish, *The Sable Arm: Negro Troops in the Union Army, 1861–1865* (1956). Black Union solders continue to attract attention. A whole volume of the

Freedom series is devoted to them: Ira Berlin, et al., eds., *The Black Military Experience* (1982). Of the many books dealing with their combat role, see especially Noah Andre Trudeau, *Like Men of War: Black Troops in the Civil War, 1862–1865* (1998). Their relations with their white officers are analyzed in Joseph T. Glatthaar, *Forged in Battle: The Civil War Alliance of Black Soldiers and White Officers* (1990). On their experiences off the battlefield, see Keith P. Wilson, *Campfires of Freedom: The Camp Life of Black Soldiers During the Civil War* (2002). Studies of specific black units recruited in the South include James G. Hollandsworth, Jr., *The Louisiana Native Guards: The Black Military Experience During the Civil War* (1995); Stephen V. Ash, *Firebrand of Liberty: The Story of Two Black Regiments That Changed the Course of the Civil War* (2008); and Richard M. Reid, *Freedom for Themselves: North Carolina's Black Soldiers in the Civil War Era* (2008). The 14 essays in John David Smith, ed., *Black Soldiers in Blue: African American Troops in the Civil War Era* (2002) examine a wide range of aspects of the soldiering experience. Only recently have the Union Navy's black sailors received their due: see Steven J. Ramold, *Slaves, Sailors, Citizens: African Americans in the Union Navy* (2002).

Only recently, too, have the distinctive experiences of black women and children in the war begun to attract the notice of historians. See especially Leslie A. Schwalm, *A Hard Fight for We: Women's Transition from Slavery to Freedom in South Carolina* (1997); James Marten, *The Children's Civil War* (1998); Noralee Frankel, *Freedom's Women: Black Women and Families in Civil War Era Mississippi* (1999); and Thavolia Glymph, *Out of the House of Bondage: The Transformation of the Plantation Household* (2008).

The forthcoming Civil War sesquicentennial will undoubtedly encourage more research on the wartime black experience. As suggested previously, certain aspects of that experience have been insufficiently explored, and others not explored at all. For one thing, we need to know more about the means by which whites kept slavery intact in the regions behind Confederate lines. A general study of rural slaves in the Confederate South, and likewise one of urban slaves, would also be helpful; so far we have only state, regional, and local studies. So, too, a general study of Border state slaves would be a welcome addition to the literature. The wartime experience of blacks who were free before the war also needs monographic exploration. So does the topic of slave removal and resettlement, which uprooted many tens of thousands of people during the war. There is much more we need to know, too, about the wartime experience of black women and children. So far no historian has focused on the experience of elderly blacks, which is surely no less worthy of attention than the children's experience. Sources for all these topics, and any number of others, are plentiful.

INDEX

ABOUT THE AUTHOR

STEPHEN V. ASH is a Professor of History at the University of Tennessee. His previously published books include *When the Yankees Came: Conflict and Chaos in the Occupied South, 1861–1865; A Year in the South: 1865: The True Story of Four Ordinary People Who Lived Through the Most Tumultuous Twelve Months in American History*; and *Firebrand of Liberty: The Story of Two Black Regiments That Changed the Course of the Civil War.* He lives in Knoxville with his wife, Jean.